'It helped me re-examine my values and direction in life – the themes covered are enough for a whole lifetime.'

– Martha O'Shea

'A deeply nourishing, restorative transformative experience ... reconnects one with heart and soul and the heart and soul of others. I challenge anyone to participate in this programme and not be transformed in some way.'

– Trish Shiel

'I found *Trellis for the Soul* enlightening, inspiring and definitely soul-nourishing. Looking back on the themes explored – stillness, Desert spirituality, wellness, care of the earth, discernment, spirituality – I realise what a treasure trove of resources is now at my fingertips.'

– Jean Kavanagh

'This programme is like no other ... Christian spirituality blended with modern, holistic depth psychology, presented in a creative way. It is more about transformation than information.'

– Sr Peggy Cronin

'Because of the richness of *Trellis for the Soul*, I am more aware of the spirit within and the spirit speaking through others. I am more aware of how stress is often created by "secondary suffering" and have learnt how to reduce it through living in the now.'

– Pat O'Neill

TRELLIS
for the Soul

A Vision of Hope for Challenging Times

MARTINA LEHANE SHEEHAN

Foreword by Mark Patrick Hederman, OSB

VERITAS

Published 2020 by
Veritas Publications
7–8 Lower Abbey Street
Dublin 1, Ireland

publications@veritas.ie
www.veritas.ie

ISBN 978-1-84730-957-0

10 9 8 7 6 5 4 3 2 1

A catalogue record for this book is available from the British Library.

Designed by Lir Mac Cárthaigh
Printed in Ireland by SPRINT-print Ltd, Dublin

Veritas books are printed on paper made from the wood pulp of managed forests. For every tree felled, at least one tree is planted, thereby renewing natural resources.

To Abina
May you never be forgotten

Contents

FOREWORD by Mark Patrick Hederman, OSB   9
A BLESSING FOR YOUR JOURNEY by Daniel J. O'Leary   13
ACKNOWLEDGEMENTS   15
INTRODUCTION   17

PART ONE
CHAPTER ONE: Created to Blossom   25
CHAPTER TWO: Discerning the Signs of the Times   35
CHAPTER THREE: Hearing the Drumbeat   43
CHAPTER FOUR: Called to the Edge   51
CHAPTER FIVE: Out with the Old: Re-wiring and Re-firing   63
CHAPTER SIX: Creating the Trellis   75
CHAPTER SEVEN: Ever Ancient, Ever New   91
Making a Contract with Yourself   104

PART TWO
CHAPTER EIGHT: Wellness and Mental Health   109
CHAPTER NINE: All of Creation: Caring for Our
     Lovely Earth   117
CHAPTER TEN: Balanced Lifestyle   127
CHAPTER ELEVEN: Soulful Living   133
CHAPTER TWELVE: Sabbath: Time to Fill the Well   141
CHAPTER THIRTEEN: Community: Healing
     and Integration   151
CHAPTER FOURTEEN: Dying to Live: Liminal Spaces   161
CHAPTER FIFTEEN: Stillness, Meditation, Healing   167
CHAPTER SIXTEEN: Creative Expression: The Colour of
     Your Soul   175
CHAPTER SEVENTEEN: Launching Your Rule of Life   183

Foreword

SOME PEOPLE THINK THAT MONASTIC LIFE IS FOR THE FEW, the strong, the holy; in fact, monastic life was designed for the weak, the craven and the addictive. In the sixth century, when civilisation, as it was then known in the West, had collapsed with the fall of the Roman Empire and the Western world had been reduced to chaos and barbarity, a young man, now known as St Benedict, decided to write a guidebook for those who wanted to return to some kind of healthy living and sobriety in body, mind and spirit. His 'little rule for beginners' has survived for over sixteen hundred years.

Martina Lehane Sheehan has undertaken a similar task for the twenty-first century as St Benedict did in the sixth century and, in my view, has done us all a comparable service.

This book provides a useful guide towards freedom for those who are living in frustration with conventional structures, yet are seeking a satisfying spiritual life. The book combines wisdom from every possible source. It is a very impressive and timely presentation.

We all know what we would like to be like. We make New Year's resolutions on an annual basis to achieve such outcomes. We have a goal in mind, we prepare tools to help us succeed, and we make efforts to inspire ourselves by keeping the ideal picture of ourselves constantly in mind. Dreams of reaching the finishing line are given up so easily. Nevertheless, we sign up for weekend courses, conferences and workshops, all of which guarantee to make mystics out of us within a month.

So, what's so different about this book, *Trellis for the Soul* by Martina Lehane Sheehan? Martina knows how long our New Year's resolutions usually last. More importantly, she knows why they don't last. And most importantly of all, she knows how to make them into a way of life. Like St Benedict, Martina has a pretty shrewd idea about what we're made of, so this book is not an airy-fairy fantasy about providing us with wings. The author has read widely and has given many courses on the programme she is presenting. Her understanding is not her own concoction. It is the deep and painstaking distillation of wisdoms from the past, teachings from any and every religious practice on the planet, and input and feedback from the many who have attended and benefitted from what she has prepared over the years, and which she is presenting here in book form.

This book explains how, far from being predetermined either by our environment or our genes, we are provided with an adaptive plasticity that awaits our decisive action. This can form us into the eventual shape we choose to become. A balanced life is what we need. But who can achieve it? Who can tell us how? Martina's book is a very good 'first steps in how to balance'.

Now supposing the ultimate possibility, the goal on offer is to live forever and get our bodies, minds and spirits ready for infinity and eternity beyond space and time. Astronauts will have some notion of what it takes to get ourselves beyond the gravitational grasp of this planet, but most of us are prisoners of its gravitational pull.

Martina is offering an alternative. If you follow the instructions in this book, you can become a new person, you can become fully yourself. You can finally unlock the chains. You can take up that invitation to become a more fully resurrected person. It takes small steps, it takes time and it takes determination to allow yourself to become the fullest extent of those possibilities already programmed into your personality.

Because the world we live in is determined to keep the bar low and economic forces are latching on to our infantile need for instant gratification, we need something to motivate us, to turn on the windscreen wipers, to get us back on the road. Instead of the many quick-fix panaceas shouting their sure-fire cure-all fantasies from the billboards, I would choose this book. It is the real deal. The style is accessible and colloquial. It provides an effective and manageable programme for anyone interested in spiritual, mental and physical burgeoning.

MARK PATRICK HEDERMAN, OSB
October 2020

A Blessing for Your Journey
by *Daniel J. O'Leary*

The late and well-loved author, Daniel J. O'Leary was instrumental in the beginnings of Trellis for the Soul. I wasn't thinking of writing a book of this title but was developing an eight-week programme that could be offered to groups and individuals. After I sent him my ideas, he said, 'This needs to be published.' Unfortunately, he wasn't alive to see its unfolding, but he wrote the following blessing a short time before he began 'dancing towards his death'. I offer it to you as a blessing for your journey in creating your own trellis for the soul.

May you stay strong and persevering,
courageous and wholehearted in your
commitment to your vision.
May this journey be kept free from all harm,
filled only with new love, new belonging and a
new incarnation of God's beautiful presence.
May no false hearts pass through this
threshold of truth. May love be always stronger
than fear, light stronger than shadows.
May you have eyes to see the face of Christ in
every face before you. May you always let the
breeze of the *Ruah* Spirit blow your heart wide
open to endless love.

DANIEL J. O'LEARY, 2018

Acknowledgements

Many thanks to Leeann, Pam, Lir, Vivek, and all at Veritas Publications for all the work they put into this production. When we write a book, we are allowing many voices to come through us; those who have touched our paths and hearts. This calls me to give thanks for our beautiful extended Ruah Community, those who join us in our home and online. It is in gratitude to family and friends, who are a gift in my life; you know who you are! I also want to acknowledge those whose shoulders I am standing on, those who have passed/crossed the veil but continue to guide and strengthen. And, of course, thank you to my husband, Pat, a true trellis for my soul.

Introduction

THIS BOOK IS DESIGNED TO LEAD YOU ON A PATHWAY towards a more soul-directed and flourishing way of life. Within, you will be offered a spiritual vision that will help you to cultivate more resilience, balance, stillness, creativity and purpose. It will heighten your capacity towards authentically aligning yourself with your values, helping you to place what matters most to you at the centre. In helping you to listen to the longings of the soul, it will take you off autopilot and lead you softly into your heart and into your life.

Trellis for the Soul can be seen as a reflective read or as a journey to be embarked upon actively, on your own or with others. The themes explored in this book are born of the responses to a listening process in which we asked participants to express what they felt were the essentials for a soulful and flourishing life. The responses were collated and the book was ready to go when the Covid-19 pandemic hit. Suddenly, we were all behind closed doors and life was cancelled for many weeks. Publishing a book was the last thing on my mind, especially after a family member and a few close friends contracted the deadly virus and life as we knew it got turned upside down.

A crisis often carries an invitation to rethink what is working and not working in our lives, nudging us towards making new maps. Then taoiseach (prime minister) of Ireland Leo Varadkar was perhaps recognising this when, during a speech about the Covid-19 lockdown in March

2020, he spoke of 'what we have lost, what we have learned, what we have gained'.

It will take a lot of discernment to sift through what we have lost, learned and gained. The destabilising and heartbreaking accounts of whom and what we lost streamed into our living rooms each evening in the news headlines. The loss of life, the rise in numbers contracting the virus, the economic downturn and the uncertainty around the future pulled the rug from under us all. We did not, however, hear as much of what we were learning and gaining. Maybe we discovered that, while part of us craves certainty and permanency, there is a deeper place, beneath the surface, where we can find beauty and wisdom even when things fall apart. I, for one, despite some really difficult challenges, still look back rather wistfully at the 'lockdown days' when we walked the roads, pausing, listening to birdsong, saluting neighbours, noticing the arrival of every new flower or bud. Though untethered, unravelled and stripped of all certainty, many discovered how to dwell in a new rhythm and found a resilience that rose from the ashes of what had been lost.

The absence of traffic and overhead planes gifted us with a new silence, interrupted occasionally by the beep of a phone, 'I'm going to the shop. Do you need anything?' People asked one another how they were – and even waited for the answer. We knew now that we were all in kinship with one another and with all of creation. Many tended gardens and grew veg, and noticed the small miracles we had all been rushing past. The elderly and vulnerable were checked in on. Celebrities became less significant as new heroes emerged; we clapped at our doors, on roads and streets for these 'earth angels' working in hospitals, tending those afflicted with the virus. Vulnerability became palpable, which made the present moment more precious and 'slow time' offered unexpected treasures.

The gods of busyness and the voodoos of competition paused for a while, while we tried to live with the unknown and navigate the rhythm of the way of the soul.

Each time I saw the notice 'Stay at home', another mantra kept echoing: 'Stay in your cell.' This was what the desert dwellers of the third and fourth centuries taught us. 'Stay in your cell, and your cell will teach you everything,' said those who fled busy lives to inhabit an uncluttered and simple rhythm of life in the desert. The summer of 2020 (and to a lesser degree the autumn and winter) provided a type of desert where the usual escape routes were inaccessible; our routines, roles, schedules and strategies dismantled. For a few weeks, we were all like the Desert monks of long ago.

As I continued my counselling practice via Zoom and telephone, I listened to many speak of needing new supports, rhythms and practices. We all knew already that our planet had been calling us to a different rhythm of life, as had the increase in mental health difficulties, but, for many, it was the curveball of the pandemic that awakened a deeper search to find ways to reconnect with soul, with one another, and with all of creation. Together we explored what would help and, to my delight, a lot of the findings that I had been exploring and writing about in *Trellis for the Soul* were truly coming alive. As difficult as lockdown was at so many levels, most said they did not want to go back to the old 'normal'. People did not want to return to being breathless, so wired and tired that they barely tasted life.

I asked many people what was helping them to sustain some measure of inner stability and peace in these uncertain times. Interestingly, the responses very much correlated with research findings in the field known as the 'science of happiness', where the main contributors to well-being are considered to be: living in the present moment; making choices according to our deepest values; practising gratitude, compassion and present-moment living; fostering social connections/community; practising a spirituality that gives meaning; engagement in what contributes to the common good.

In *Trellis for the Soul*, these themes are interwoven with a synthesis of modern psychology, as well as some ancient wisdom drawn from many sources. Monastic rhythms, with their emphasis on stability, balance and trust, offer treasures for these times. We will, therefore, explore how we might create a contemporary interpretation of what in monastic settings is called a 'rule of life'. In this context, however, it is not an imposed rule that restricts, but one that aligns us with our highest and deepest desire for fullness of life.

'The trellis is a lifesaver,' many reported, after they had engaged in a recent *Trellis for the Soul* transformational programme online. So much so that numerous small groups have formed, nationally and internationally, with the intention of continuing the journey of nourishing and caring for the soul.

And so, in engaging with this book, you will be benefiting from what has already been tried and tested by the many who have made their own unique applications from what I have written in this book. People's responses and applications simply took my breath away. And, so, I hope that as you journey through this book, you too will be gifted with something that takes your breath away.

HOW TO BENEFIT FROM THIS BOOK

The book you are now holding is more than a self-help tool. In sprinkling contemporary psychological insights with timeless spiritual wisdom, it offers a vision for anyone who longs for soul nourishment and inspiration in navigating everyday living.

While the spiritual dimension delicately draws from the Christian contemplative and other mystical traditions, it will yield something meaningful for those of any or no faith allegiance. It does not seek to squeeze old traditions into new realities, but encourages whatever is *real, authentic and life-giving to grow and flourish again from the roots.*

In part one, there is an exploration of the present signs of the times and the hunger of the soul in contemporary living. This is followed by an exploration of how an *intentional way of life* can be a helpful response to the presenting needs of contemporary seekers. You will uncover limiting beliefs that may have gotten wired into your consciousness. You will then be introduced to the possibility of a new holistic lifestyle choice for yourself, one which becomes an anchor in helping you to prioritise, clarify and create more balance and aliveness, even during limiting or challenging external circumstances. You will be helped to create a sanctuary of inner stability, strength and compassion. In chapter five, for example, we will be exploring a commitment towards embracing our imperfections through creating a practice based on non-violence and compassion towards self and others. Many of us have become arthritic in spirit as a result of rules that are oppressive, and so we will look at how we can release those unhelpful and limiting old rules, and in letting them go we will retrieve lost parts of ourselves, resuscitating some forgotten dreams. We will explore how to declutter what clogs the soul and prevents us from living a more value-based, creative and balanced life.

In part two, following a brief outline of a template for soulful living, you will be guided to extract whatever resonates most deeply with yourself. You will be aligning all of this with your own everyday life. Our evolutionary wiring, and sometimes our early life experiences, leads us to have a stronger leaning towards the negative in our lives. Most of us tend to more readily count our mistakes or list those things undone than to count our positive qualities or, indeed, to count our blessings. To combat this we will explore some supportive practices that help us flourish. We will explore ways in which we can build habits of savouring what is good in our lives – and in ourselves. This becomes an antidote to what many people nowadays describe as 'living on empty'.

While the writing, in places, draws from what I have learnt through over twenty-five years of practice as a counsellor/psychotherapist and a retreat facilitator, the deepest insights will emerge from you, the reader. So, let there be spaces for reflection as you read; this will offer you opportunities to pause and drink from the well of your inner wisdom, helping in the liberation of your own intuition and creativity.

There are some journaling prompts/soul questions and suggestions at the end of each chapter. I am an avid believer that when we write something down, we begin to see it through a different lens. We sometimes find ourselves saying things like 'Oh I never knew that' after we have written something down. So, while it is tempting to skip over these parts, trust me, engaging with them can be a rewarding commitment. Try, therefore, not to see yourself as a passive reader, but with pen and paper, jot down insights that may help in building your own unique trellis for the soul.

So, dear reader, I look forward to being with you on this journey, where I will act as your gentle nag. (I'm good at that!) You will hear this nagging voice whenever I direct the spotlight on how we might lose perseverance and become out of kilter with our values. (I say 'we' because I, too, will be engaging in the challenges.) You will be nagged into creating a vision that will refresh and renew you in times of tiredness, uplifting your spirit and imbuing an 'ordinary' life with meaning, transcendence and beauty. All of this will help you discover, and recover, the distance you may have travelled from yourself, the ground of your being. Here, you will find yourself moving forward from cramped places that have grown too small for your soul. So, let's fasten our seat belts and begin! My hope is that on this journey, you will eventually hear not my directions or my voice, but your own – calling you from the unquenchable light of your own being.

> *I wish I could show you,*
> *When you are lonely or in darkness,*
> *The Astonishing Light*
> *Of your own Being.*
> (HAFIZ)

PART ONE

You wander from room to room
Hunting for the diamond necklace
That is already around your neck.
(RUMI)

CHAPTER ONE
Created to Blossom

SOME TIME AGO, A GARDEN DESIGNER VISITED OUR GARDEN. I don't remember much of his advice, but I do remember him looking at a little limp rose, pausing for a while, then saying in a low voice, 'She's not happy here. She needs more space. She's hungry. She needs nourishment, a bigger space. She wants to be free.' Then, in a louder, more emphatic voice, he exclaimed, 'She has outgrown this container.' (He was referring to the expensive flowerpot we had carefully chosen only months earlier.) He looked at the rose again and said with sudden realisation, 'She needs a trellis.' I thought it was a contradiction that he had earlier said, 'She wants to be free', yet now he is telling us to pin her to a trellis. I considered the trellis to be something restrictive, so I vehemently resisted. I decided I knew better, so I dismissed the trellis idea but took the rest of his advice.

As suggested, we changed her pot, giving her a new spacious one that allowed her roots to go deep into the soil. We added good nutrition and a lot of manure. Job done, I told myself: she is no longer confined and is now wild and free with plenty of space to grow in whatever direction she wants.

And yes, she did grow, wild and free, but some weeks later, we noticed she was starting to droop and keel over, unable to support herself. In fact, with every passing gust of wind, she was blown in all directions.

Eventually, and reluctantly, we did what he had suggested: we made a trellis. We fastened the rose to this carefully structured framework. She leaned against it as if to say, 'Ah, that's better.' After a few weeks, she began to lift up her bowed head, showed her little pink face and moved her arms outwards and upwards, beautifully supported in her natural growth towards the light.

INGREDIENTS FOR BLOSSOMING

I continued to reflect on the three ingredients that the garden designer had mentioned: nutrition for her soil, a bigger space and a supportive structure. Were these three essentials present in my life or did I also need to be repotted into a bigger space?

I began to notice the places and situations, where, like the rose, I too was a bit squeezed with too many to-do lists, resulting in an often breathless hurrying from one thing to another. Like many others, I frequently found myself talking about being too busy and lacking space between engagements. The hurried rhythm of life was becoming a hazardous habit for myself and, apparently, for so many others. Chasing some imaginary finishing line, we were all becoming increasingly dehydrated and under-nourished at soul level. Eventually, I responded to this by changing work practices and altering commitments.

Excitedly, I looked forward to having more time for creative activities and time to enjoy some of those many books I never got around to reading. I especially looked forward to having plenty of time for writing. Surprisingly, though, this free time wasn't as life-giving as I had hoped; in fact, I found myself becoming unmotivated, listless, unfocused and drooping in energy, a bit like the rose. I was identifying with what the Desert monks referred to as accidie/acedia, which is a state of listlessness, apathy, sloth. I recognised that a blank page or a blank day wasn't as exhilarating as I had expected. I needed some kind of supportive structures or practices. A more holistic rhythm of life was necessary, so I finally admitted that what I needed was exactly what I resisted: a trellis for the soul.

I began to share this idea with a few companions and it resonated deeply with them. They too began to make commitments to live more intentionally and with more balance.

Maybe, like me, you find even the mention of creating a 'structure' off-putting. Maybe it creates the same reaction as the word 'dentist'! This is probably because you associate it with cramping your style and hampering the desire to go with the flow. We forget that certain structures and rhythms can actually provide the very impetus and support we need to flow and grow. They help us to move from force to source and, so, to grow into our deepest desires.

If, for a moment, you were to imagine yourself as a rose or a plant: are you blossoming, flourishing, or dried out and tired? Are you in the ground or in a container? Do you have space, or are you cramped and squeezed? Visualise your roots underground: are they nourished and thriving? Are they breathing easily, or being choked and robbed of energy by other intertwining roots? Are you planted in a place where you receive enough sunlight, so that you can blossom and share your colour with the world? What do you need to support you?

SUPPORTIVE STRUCTURES

I have to admit I find discipline difficult at almost every level of my life; however, when I began to build in a few structures with steadying commitments, such as journaling, regular meditation, scriptural reflection, intentional practising of compassion, gratitude, and reverence for creation, I found an increase in creativity, focus and sense of direction.

The commitment to a more intentional rhythm of life became a very important ingredient on the trellis. Only much later did I discover that there was a monastic practice called a 'rule of life', a way of living which aligns your values and deepest intentions with supportive commitments. This seemed very similar to what I had been referring to as a 'trellis for the soul'.

I was exploring this way of life for many years before I discovered that there were other people around the globe also beginning to feel the need to create lifestyle changes, more rhythmic, even monastic ways of stepping off the treadmill of speed, consumerism, individualism and accumulation. The world pandemic has led many to integrate their values into more holistic, contemplative practices in daily life. I continue to meet them especially through my work in counselling, psychotherapy and whenever I am facilitating workshops and retreats. I am privileged to meet many people at a very transparent and authentic level where they say the 'real things' and encounter the big questions. More and more, I hear people say that they are searching for space and are outgrowing some old ways of being that have become too small for them.

BENEATH THE NOISE

In the listening process, I asked many people about 'soul hunger' and how they experience it today. I asked questions such as: where do you identify a lack of balance in your life? What nourishes your soul? What kind of structures/practices do you feel people are searching for today? Many said they felt they were just doing the daily rounds, tick-boxing their days, but low-grade anxiety and uncertainty were preventing them from savouring their lives. Some said they were drifting along more by default than by design. Busy, distracted and time poor, many felt numbed-out and unable to feel or taste any real joy. One lady described feeling as if she was living on borrowed time, waking tired each morning, checking her to-do list, restraining her impatience with those around her and just getting through with lots of caffeine, quick-fix carbs on the go, while hoping any extra demands wouldn't tip her over the edge. Phew, that sounds exhausting! One gentleman, feeling so tired from living in a continuous noisy mind and noisy life, described himself as becoming increasingly 'cut off from the sunlight of his spirit'.

They were all, in some way, describing a life where they were surviving, but not thriving – existing, but not blossoming. All identified that there was a deeper set of yearnings rumbling underground. In the listening process, each of the following was mentioned as important:

- An ability to live more in the present moment.
- A balanced lifestyle, for the sake of mental health, well-being and the common good.
- A holistic, integrated spirituality, living in kinship with community and all of creation.
- A desire to develop purpose and passion for living.
- A rhythm of life that would offer soul-care, not just for ourselves, but also for others, our planet, future generations and for those at the margins.

SUPPORTIVE TRELLIS

To allow oneself to be carried away by a multitude of conflicting concerns, to surrender to too many demands, to commit oneself to too many projects, to want to help everyone in everything, is to succumb to the violence of our times. (THOMAS MERTON)

On listening, it became clear that serenity or creativity cannot exist when we are too tightly packed with schedules and plans, but neither can it emerge through big chunks of unsupported, aimless free time. That is why we need a balance between some creative space and supportive nourishing structures; in other words, a more holistic way of living. We need something that offers us both stability and mobility.

I don't know if I was excited or disappointed to hear one person say he needed some kind of 'plant support stick', or 'trellis'! I was excited on one hand, because it confirmed the concept I had been exploring, but disappointed also because I thought the trellis was my *original* idea. (The ego always likes a look-in.) Maybe this confirms that none of us is totally original; instead, we are all tuning into some deeper collective wisdom, where we are connected at root level with one another and with everything that lives and breathes. Either way, I am very glad that the image of the trellis was given to me from the wise gardener that day.

THE POWER OF INTENTION

Go confidently in the direction of your dreams. Live the life you've imagined. As you simplify your life, the laws of the universe will be simple. (HENRY DAVID THOREAU)

Foundational to creating any soul trellis or lifestyle change is setting an intention. This is the energy that infuses our actions, choices and habits. In each situation we can ask, 'Is my intention here born out of love or born out of fear?' When my intention is based on fear, I might find myself in habits of people-pleasing, manipulating, controlling and selling out on my values. Fear will drive me to seek external power; however, when I base my intention on love, I will be drawing from internal power. Here I will not be a servant to the ego, but will be serving the soul – that part of us that always seeks the deepest and the highest good. Following the voice of the soul brings a meaningful context and a value to the most ordinary experiences; it offers a more expansive vibrational energy to all of life.

At the end of our recent *Trellis for the Soul* transformational programme, each person presented their rule of life, which they had created throughout the year. One of our participants, Mary, presented her interpretation of 'intentional living'. She described how, in her work as a consultant psychiatrist, it is easy to 'become governed by the need to protect oneself in fear of litigation, complaints, etc.' She now sets her intention at the beginning of each day to live by the value of the 'highest good' of her patients. She said that even though it can be difficult, she intentionally chooses to make decisions from 'conscience, rather than from the need to self-defend'. I greatly admire Mary's choice here, because it is indeed a brave decision to choose to serve the energy of the soul rather than the ego, to serve love rather than fear. It is one thing to live spiritual values in an environment where others share similar ideals, but it can be very difficult to choose the way of the soul in unchartered territories, or where a very different world view dominates.

DRAWN TO THE SACRED

Through the listening process, it was clear that nobody really wants to sleepwalk through their life; many are awakening to a cosmic consciousness and an awareness of our interconnection and interdependence with the whole web of life. While there seems to be a reduction, in recent times, in those subscribing to organised religion, there is an irrepressible sense of spirituality in the human psyche. The search isn't so much for mindfulness as for soulfulness. This hunger for the sacred is increasingly obvious in the surprising number of people beginning to explore the ways of reflective living and cultivating compassionate presence to self and all that we share this planet with. There seems to be a new call to excavate ancient wisdom and monastic rhythms and to integrate these practices into contemporary language.

Pat, my husband, and I did some discernment around what might support a new rhythm of life, for ourselves, as well as for those who had expressed a similar need. We felt some kind of transition was soon to arrive, where, like the rose, we were going to be 'repotted', whatever that might mean. Be careful what you pray for: we both ended up resigning from our places of employment and making a complete inventory of our lives (more about this later). While you may not wish to make any drastic choices like this, you may discover that you have an inner desire to be repotted in other ways. Perhaps you are seeking a lifestyle change, a decluttering of the old, a new sense of spaciousness. Perhaps you realise that you want to let go of the confinements of adapting to external expectations, or maybe you have outgrown a container where you have, for too long, been 'playing small'. Maybe you feel the call to finally take up your full and unique place in the universe.

We all have an inner desire for fullness of life, but it rarely emerges of its own accord; it usually has to be called into being. The process by which we do this is sometimes called 'creative visualisation'. Of course, we are visualising all the time, but more often than not, it is an unconscious picture of what we do not want, based on our fears, rather than focusing on what we do want, based on our values.

The brain is constantly sending subliminal images, but we have to channel those many nuanced messages. Christian mystic Meister Eckhart (1260–1328) suggested that when the soul wishes to experience something, she throws an image of the desired picture out before her and enters into her own image. You might argue: why not just be spontaneous and wait to see what unfolds? However, while you do need to develop a capacity to trust the flow of life, you also need to be proactive in co-creating what is truly important to you; otherwise you assign away your own creative capacities. Remember, when everything is a priority, in effect, nothing is a priority!

CREATIVE VISUALISATION
For where your treasure is, there your heart will be also. (MT 6:21)

Albert Einstein said, 'Imagination is the preview of life's coming attractions.' Imagining life's possibilities is not just indulgent, passive daydreaming based on mere wishing and hoping. When Alice in Wonderland came to a fork on the road, she asked the Cheshire Cat which route she should take. His response was to ask her where she wanted to go. Alice said she didn't know, to which the cat replied, 'Then it doesn't matter which way you go.' It is the same for us: if we don't really know where we want to go, or where our treasure lies and what is really important, we will flounder around in every direction. When we come to that fork on the road, we have to not only choose to follow a path, but we will also have to choose the path we will *not* follow.

Envisioning a picture of your pearl of great price, and what you really value, is not a directing of energies into something so future-based that you lose connection with where you are now. It is more a conscious, intentional envisioning of a life well lived. The area of the brain responsible for joy and fulfilment is known as the hippocampus. Here there are two neurotransmitters, dopamine and serotonin, which can be activated through the internal positive pictures we create for ourselves.

So, before we go further let's pause so you can reflect on your own soul hunger and your desire to blossom and flourish. This is important because when you shrink and dilute your own uniqueness and lock yourself away where the world cannot find you, there is an immeasurable loss to humanity.

Maybe you can begin by taking a blank page and writing these simple but profound questions: What truly brings me alive? How might this aliveness be expressed in my life at present? Take a few minutes to visualise yourself living a balanced life, true to your values, honouring your need for rest and stillness, while having a sense of contribution and service to the interconnected web of life. What would this look like? Allow all your senses to create this picture, envisioning where you are, and who else is in this picture. What pace of daily life would you be committed to? What social activities would you engage in/not engage in? What would you be doing more of? What would you do less of? Keep writing and sketching until you want to stop.

PRESS PAUSE

Remember, we cannot find balance, serenity or creativity when we are too tightly packed with schedules and plans, but neither can we with big chunks of unsupported, aimless free time.

Creating Your Trellis

Jot down what is staying with you from this chapter. Where might there be a personal invitation for you?

If your life were portrayed in a film, what title would it have? Are you in the leading role or is somebody else?

Have you been playing the part that represents who you really are, or have you been acting the part others have assigned to you?

What emotion does this film evoke in you? How do you feel those watching it might describe your role?

Have some fun writing a really compelling ending to the film.

Having thrown your desired vision out before you, identify one habitual thing that presently takes you away from this compelling vision. (It might be avoidant behaviour such as over-commitment, too many to-do lists, self-criticism or habits of giving away your power.) Identify one small step to help choreograph and align your habits and actions towards the vision you created above. You might, for example, start off by deciding to carve out a short time each day to slow the mind and simply be still and listen to the heart's deeper longings.

CHAPTER TWO
Discerning the Signs of the Times

IF YOU ENQUIRE OF PEOPLE HOW THEY ARE, MOST WILL TELL you how things are going at work or how busy they are. In our adrenaline-pumped lives, we have been forgetting how to connect and tell each other how we truly are. Many, in sheer exhaustion and burnout, have for years been living at a pace that they never really chose and find themselves asking, 'How did I get here?' Maybe this is why there seems to be a collective conscious cry to rediscover something deeper, something that lies beneath the daily noise. Even though freedom can sometimes feel scarier than our familiar prisons, and even though 'birthing pain' can hurt, the soul will not be silenced. The collective soul is waking up and telling us that despite progress on a variety of levels, we have, in many ways, become estranged from ourselves, from one another and from Mother Earth.

NEW THRESHOLDS
Before this global pandemic, most of us were speeding along, keeping the show on the road. Then, because of an invisible virus, we heard the screeching sound of the brakes as we were forced to reduce to a slower pace. We met our vulnerability, our impermanence and our collective anxiety. We also glimpsed how closely connected we all are. 'We are all in this together' was written on notices everywhere

and, deep down, we knew we had to choose what is truly important in life. We discovered the many subtle miracles and everyday beauties that we had rushed past.

We have, for a long time, been saturated with overwhelming consumer choices, yet many are expressing a type of 'choice fatigue' and feeling an isolated and individualistic lethargy. Despite the numerous conveniences around us and online, many suffer a kind of 'purpose anxiety' and beneath the surface they long for a sense of meaning. As wonderful as technology is – and it certainly offers invaluable gifts – it cannot listen to your loneliness, it cannot provide spaces for deeper soul nourishment, it cannot walk with you hand in hand in befriending the mystery of your life, and it cannot touch your fears when facing your mortality. None of us likes uncertainty. We like to know the plot and how the story will end. We would like to be told exactly when we will have freedom from uncertainty and an economically secure world again. Yes, if only we had a crystal ball and knew the date and time we would all be back in charge of our lives, like little gods. Society encourages us to place a high value on always being on top of our game and, of course, always having a contingency plan. This emphasis on 'bigger, better, faster' has surely underpinned much of our modern, social and ecological issues.

We seem to be at a threshold. The 'thresh' in the word 'threshold' relates to the separation of the grain from the husk, a shedding of the exterior husks in order to gather and save the central essence. I think this threshold is actually exciting because it asks us to sift through and discard what no longer works, while seeking to retain what is authentic and essential for living. We know now that we can no longer ignore the important task of soul-care for each other, our planet and ourselves.

TIRED OF BEING TIRED

Of those we interviewed, quite a few said they wanted to drop the constant overdrive from their lives. They agreed that it is good to have goals to reach towards, but identified that a lot of the pressure is based on fear – of not having enough and of not being enough. Uncertainty and fear can make us push and pull until exhausted; our insecurity can drive us to push our opinions, possessions, reputation and our accomplishments.

Barrelling through the days, many of us report living 'good, but distracted' lives, not lacking in soul but often too preoccupied to feed its hungers. There is actually a greater chance of suffering burnout from frustration, repressed emotions and lack of inspiration than from any physical overwork.

'Ah no, I can't, I'm exhausted, burnt out,' I replied when I was invited to write a play back in the year 2000; however, after I had written and staged it, the tiredness was a distant memory. Despite the long hours of travel and rehearsals, I was firing on all cylinders, simply because I was engaged in something that activated energy rather than draining it. We become drained when we follow the ego and all its fears but we become energised when we are aligned with soul. Scripture advises that 'those who wait for the Lord shall renew their strength, they shall mount up with wings like eagles, they shall run and not be weary, they shall walk and not faint' (Is 40:31).

The energising of inner creativity, soul wisdom and intuition is often neglected when we only use the left brain in constant fact-finding and dualistic problem-solving. When we access the right brain, we see a broader, more compassionate picture and we see endless creative possibilities. This is also true at a collective level and has consequences for every area of life, especially when it comes to good leadership.

RIPPLES

We hear news each day that reminds us that planet earth is in danger. Homelessness increases, economic uncertainty looms, racism and collective trauma affects us and illness threatens us. We can feel helpless hearing about these continuous ripples of danger and bad news; however, we need to stay mindful that we, too, are continually creating ripples. Each day, we can create a ripple. It can be one where hope is reborn, where our presence brings healing, and where we refuse to subscribe to a throw-away culture. We can communicate through our way of being and our way of seeing that, even amidst difficulties, life is precious and sacred. We can, despite the depressing daily news, continue to witness to how privileged we are to be alive in this beautiful world. Our gratitude and compassion create vibrational healing ripples around us. We discover this mostly when we become still and intentionally listen to the small voice beneath the noise.

WITHOUT A MAP

Most of those who participated in our listening process were around the mid-life stage but some were younger and some much older. Surprisingly, age didn't actually make a major difference in terms of the expressed common search and hungers of the heart. Ageing is obviously not the only way the soul nudges itself into attending to the spiritual dimension of life. In the final lines of his play *Krapp's Last Tape* (1958), Samuel Beckett writes, 'Perhaps my best years are gone. When there was a chance of happiness. But I wouldn't want them back. Not with the fire in me now. No, I wouldn't want them back.' The *fire in us now* isn't counting how many years we have lived. It is more interested in what those years have taught us and how we can continue to offer our bright wisdom to our world.

It was very exciting to hear so many people express that they are no longer satisfied with merely marking off the days or building up their empires; instead, they are beginning to explore the legacies they want to leave behind. People are beginning to want more – but not more stuff. They want more quality and texture in their daily lives, and less of what drains their creative juices. Almost everybody we questioned mentioned something about his or her concern for creation. One person said that she does not want to be 'part of a generation that will be remembered for destroying the planet through over-consumption'. Many want to reconnect with simplicity of heart and lifestyle, and want to live the rhythm of sacral time.

Many mentioned how important it is to take care of mental health in uncertain times. They were excited to learn of new discoveries in neuroscience and how we can alter neural habits. Some people said they are beginning to declutter, throwing out some old uniforms of conformity to societal pressures. In conclusion, there seems to be a lot of people who are no longer content to walk on the slippery ground of materialism and speed, with continuous insecurity gaping underfoot.

WHERE WE LEAST EXPECT

In the Old Testament, when Jacob awoke from his sleep, he discovered that 'the Lord is in this place – and I did not know' (Gn 28:16). Maybe it is difficult to see where God is in 'this place' at this present time, but it is our time, the only time and place over which the Spirit can now hover.

We must choose not a glorified past nor an imagined perfect future, but simply remain on tiptoe, excitedly listening for what is emerging right now, right here. There are no 'good old days'. We must know we are accompanied and supported through these in-between times. We have the choice to see everything as disaster or, instead, like Jacob of the Old Testament, we can awake from our sleep and begin to see that Divine Providence is, indeed, in this place.

The eyes of the soul can enter places where the logical mind cannot. Through these eyes, we can begin to look to the past with reverence, look to today with awareness, and look to the future with hope. While this may draw us into unfamiliar landscapes, where we find ourselves plunged into the unknown, something in us knows that we cannot go back, no more than the butterfly in the cocoon can return to being a caterpillar.

HOPE IN SHIFTING LANDSCAPES

If we can look around as our inner and outer landscapes start to shift like tectonic plates on the earth's crust, perhaps we will see that something new is trying to break through. There are a lot of exciting 'earthquakes' presently happening in human consciousness, whether they are initiating a type of ecological revolution or pushing against laws of oppression and consumerism.

In these shifting landscapes, we often feel as if we are on a knife-edge because what serves our ego, what society expects of us, is often at variance with the emerging longings of the soul. It is often when we find ourselves in the desert of transitional times that we begin to yield to an alternative rhythm and pace of living. Here, we ask a different set of questions, important and potentially transformative ones, such as: Am I living what is truly important? Do I find myself selling out on my values for the sake of expediency?

FREEDOM TO CHOOSE

No matter what our present circumstances, or what society expects of us, life can be more than a mindless meandering through the motions of exhausting, numbing routines. We have, according to the father of psychoanalysis, Sigmund Freud, a life instinct and a death instinct operating in us. While we have to respect the full array of human conflicts, each clamouring for our attention, we do have the capacity to strengthen our life instinct. Our death instinct is fed through pessimism, cynicism and postponement of the simple initiatives that bring us alive. Personally, I consider myself to be the queen of procrastination. I have wardrobes of reasons why I put off things until tomorrow. If you would like to learn how to procrastinate, trust me, I am well qualified to teach you! I am gradually coaching myself to take small steps in the present moment instead of imagining I will change it all 'some fine day'. I am gradually learning to cultivate more inner resilience through learning to endure short-term discomfort for the sake of a long-term treasure/ value.

Viktor E. Frankl, the renowned Austrian neurologist, psychiatrist and author of *Man's Search for Meaning* (1946), witnessed the most horrific conditions and cruelty in the

Nazi concentration camps. During his imprisonment, he wrote his observations, concluding that no matter the circumstances in which we find ourselves, we always have choices. He says, 'Everything can be taken from a man but one thing: the last of the human freedoms, to choose one's attitude in any given set of circumstances, to choose one's own way.'[1]

He himself had discovered an inner resilience, so much so that even as they tried to destroy him, he discovered that he actually had more freedom than his torturers: 'Every day, every hour, offered the opportunity to make a decision, a decision which determined whether you would or would not submit to those powers which threatened to rob you of your very self, your inner freedom.'[2]

While most of us, hopefully, are not being tortured or imprisoned on a daily basis, perhaps there are other influences taking away our freedom. Frankl reminds us that we do not need to 'submit to those powers' that rob us of freedom. We can, for example, choose to unsubscribe from excessive fear of the future and catastrophic stories of what might or could happen. We can unsubscribe from the relentless self-bullying of the inner critic in its insistence that we buy into social comparison and follow the status quo. We can choose the 'last of the human freedoms' and say yes to stepping outside our mental prison doors. Here we can breathe in the fresh air, where there is always the option to choose one's own way.

PRESS PAUSE

Remember, there are a lot of ripples that we cannot change in the world, but we can have an impact through the ripples we ourselves create.

---

1. Viktor E. Frankl, *Man's Search for Meaning*, London: Random House, 2004, p. 75.
2. Ibid.

Creating Your Trellis

Jot down what is staying with you from this chapter. Where might there be a personal invitation for you?

On one side of a page, write down a list of those things that you have the power to change. On the other side, write a list of what you do not have power to change, right now.

Choose one small action from your 'power to change' list and commit to taking that step. This will give you back a sense of empowerment.

Choose one issue from your 'unable to change right now' list (this might be the actions, behaviour or choices of others); see if, with acceptance, you can choose your attitude around it. Perhaps you can release control around the outcome and peacefully surrender all fixed expectations. This will lessen the spiral of internal reactivity and give you back a huge amount of energy and peace of mind.

CHAPTER THREE
Hearing the Drumbeat

Each day in our world beauty is born anew, it rises transformed through the storms of history. Values always tend to reappear under new guises, and human beings have arisen time after time from situations that seemed doomed.
(*EVANGELII GAUDIUM*, 276)

EVERY AGE HAS EXPLORED THE BIGGER QUESTIONS IN WAYS peculiar to itself. People have always attempted to put expression on the yearnings of the human spirit. Embedded in each of us is the search for what animates and sustains all of life. We can easily lose sight of the beauty of our embryonic inner spirit. We frequently blur it with toxic junk food for the soul, bingeing excessively on social media, focusing on catastrophic news, negative dramas and self-shaming comparisons. Despite all of this, the search for a deeper beauty and transcendence continues to create a kind of gnawing that stalks the soul. This holy restlessness often best expresses itself through dreams or through a poem, a piece of music or a piece of art. It can be so subtle and wild that it defies our attempts to systematise or define it. It is easy, so, to see why the ego has no interest in spiritual matters.

There are changes in the understanding and practices of 'spiritual living' in every historical era. These are often extroverted into changes of attitude in social, political and economic spheres. Many agree that the word 'spirituality' can mean just about anything right now, and does not necessarily point to anything related to a faith, a higher power or the evolution of any higher consciousness. This leaves some people without a map or a blueprint to follow. While some express a sense of being lost in all of this obscurity, others say they are excited by the search for new possibilities and a more expanded understanding of what animates and gives meaning to life. New scientific discoveries around the story of the universe seem to be strengthening a sense of spirituality for many. As one participant of the listening process – a self-professed atheist – remarked, 'I know now that there is an existence of some benevolent, creative intelligence behind it all.' However, some others deeply lament the passing of many comforting symbols around their religious beliefs. One man said, 'I feel as if everything is slipping away and changing.' On a lighter note, one young lady I interviewed described herself as 'fierce spiritual'. She went on to say, 'Don't get me wrong, I'm not a Holy Joe. I don't believe in God or anything, but I do believe in angels.' I didn't quite understand the concept of deleting God in favour of angels. I looked at her angel earrings, her angel purse, her angel tattoo and found myself, for the rest of the day, singing a line from the song 'Angels' by Robbie Williams in which the singer proclaims to be loving angels *instead*.

Theologian and contemplative scholar, Beverly Lanzetta writes, 'The monastic call is intrinsic to all people and is not confined to religious organisations or orders. It is a free call within the self, one that is born with us into the world and to which we allow allegiance.'[1] Lanzetta reminds us, 'There is nothing more natural than to affirm one's monastic nature, living in God's time, seeking transformation into the heart of reality, and loving creation with one's whole being.'[2]

While everyone has the longing and capacity to experience the beauty and mystery of the 'free call within the self', it is not easy to hear it echoing beneath the noise.

1. Beverly Lanzetta, *The Monk Within: Embracing a Sacred Way of Life*, Sebastopol, CA: Blue Sapphire Books, 2018, p. 121.
2. Ibid.

A FORCE OF LOVE

There is no neat label to describe the interrelated force of love moving in the whole universe, yet it is the very beat of our hearts. It is a visceral life force that compels us to forge a new creative drumbeat in our world. The irrepressible beat of the spirit will never cease to pulsate in the human heart, imprinting new unique callings in every era. Across history, there were always seekers who heard it and responded by fleeing the popular culture and creating a new way of life.

DRUMBEAT OF THE DESERT

I have a great interest in the desert dwellers of the third and fourth centuries. Wishing to return to grassroots Christian communities and a true following of the gospel, they left behind popular culture and the model of church of their day, which they felt was losing its prophetic edge. They chose secluded settings along the river Nile, in the deserts of Palestine, Egypt, Syria, and later in Britain and Ireland. They withdrew from cities to live more freely and to detach from the cultural and political structures of the Roman Empire. At the time, Constantine had given Christianity a privileged status and a position of power. The Desert Fathers and Mothers felt that power and prestige was not compatible with the way of Christ. Their chosen solitude and silence was not an escape, but rather a way to become better at seeing, serving and loving more deeply. Withdrawal was not, therefore, for self-preoccupation but was for the sake of offering a transformed presence to the world.

Others soon followed this new drumbeat and little villages sprang up. Much later, this Desert tradition initiated the early roots of Celtic monasticism. While they espoused a meditative way of life, the desert dwellers were often seen as suspect and considered to have heretical tendencies, and were frequently criticised by the powers that be. (That seems to be the archetypal pattern of anything new that emerges!)

RISING FROM FALLING STRUCTURES

When we look back through the ages, we notice that it is often during a time of falling structures that something new emerges. Saint Antony of Egypt (252–356), who is widely acknowledged as the founder of the Desert movement, fled the culture of the time and, alongside others, cultivated an alternative way of living. Many others fled to the hills or rural places, where they gathered to make a 'lifestyle change' relevant to their time. Today, there are again many people feeling disenfranchised and 'fleeing to the hills' to explore a more intentional way of living. When so much of society's expectation is focused on making us feel like human 'doings' instead of human beings, leaving aside those external expectations and choosing to enter into our own interiority is not easy. In the desert of our hearts, we meet ourselves; wherever we go, and wherever we turn, there we are.

When we do take time to enter into the desert places of the heart, it can be both blissful and brutal. The desert created by the Covid-19 lockdown was both blissful and brutal; the bliss of rediscovering a more reflective rhythm coupled with the brutality of loneliness and human frailty.

There are stirrings of newness becoming evident again in today's falling structures. It is heartening to see so many young people rising up in support of climate change initiatives and speaking out against inequality and prejudice in our societies and hypocrisy in political systems. There are many 'ordinary' people, doing ordinary things. They are the bringers of healing in this time of cultural and relational fragmentation. They are torchbearers and trailblazers, igniting the path for other searching souls. You are one of them, but maybe you discount the new birthings in your own soul? What might be the pay-off in not trusting your part of the Divine Dance? Perhaps you might let yourself gently answer the following:

How do I hide my light, and what might be the pay-off for doing this?
I'm afraid if I listened to inner guidance, I might ...
I distract myself because ...
If I really said yes to the wisdom of my soul, I would ...

In all of the above, you may discover there are ways in which you compensate. Perhaps by employing avoidant behaviours, such as accumulating too much stuff, spending too much time doubting yourself or habitually getting caught in other people's expectations of you. If any of these are true for you, do not judge yourself. Think of these as diversionary activities to derail you from the magnificent truth of who you are and what you can offer to the world.

TO WALK THE TALK

After I had completed the listening process, I decided that all I had to do was go off and write up the findings in a few notes, or maybe give a talk. However, an unexpected drumbeat was getting louder, announcing that the time was at hand – it was time to walk the talk.

Part of what attracted me to the spirituality of the desert was its emphasis on engaging in ministry more through a lifestyle than through words. Abba of the Desert, Isidore of Pelusium, said, 'To live without speaking is better than to speak without living. For the former who lives rightly does good even by his silence but the latter does no good even when he speaks.'

'To speak without living' doesn't convince today's seekers, in church, business or political arenas. We often preach far more effectively through what we do not say than through our words. We can give powerful witness through our lifestyle and to what and whom we devote our time. I became more convinced of this after the following incident.

It was the early nineties and I was part of a rather high-powered, professional team that went around to schools and various settings giving talks and creating quite a stir. One day we were preparing a speaking event on the theme of compassion. As one of our own younger team members had been ill for quite a while, I suggested that if we were to give this talk authentically, it might be a good idea to begin by visiting our own colleague who was bedridden. An older team member turned to me and, trying to restrain his annoyance, said, 'Martina, our job is to deliver the message, that's all, no more.' He went on to explain, 'In delivering the message, you need only be like the milkman. He just delivers the milk, but he himself doesn't have to drink the bloody thing.'

Though this incident happened many years ago, it stayed indelibly in my mind. I suppose, something in me now knows that while none of us perfectly practises what we preach, the most important thing is that we aim to do our best to *live the bloody thing*. The soul knows when there is integrity and congruence, and will only follow a drumbeat where there is some willingness to walk the talk.

In response to all of this, Pat and I felt drawn (though resistant) to begin living the vision that was slowly emerging through this new inner drumbeat. We felt drawn to create a way of life that initially we ourselves would commit to, while also creating space for those who felt drawn to join us. We knew community would have to be a key factor and would appeal to those who are tired of materialistic and individualistic dead ends, those searching for an oasis in the desert of these transitional times.

We felt we could not just 'white-knuckle' it alone but would only find integration through interacting and collaborating with others. We would not wait until we had a perfect vision before we would 'show up'. There is always lurking that false belief that we have to sanitise our personalities before we risk anything. Nothing could be further from the truth; we just need to become aware and honest in all our contradictions and shadows and, in doing so, we give permission to other fearful souls to also become aware and honest. Together we become bread, broken and blessed for one another.

This was the scary part, bringing our imperfect selves and our uncertain and incomplete dreams out of hiding. The fear of criticism is very real when you do not have a clear blueprint – yet, the path can only be made by walking.

None of this is really about big gestures and big numbers applauding us. You can become an agent of transformation without even leaving your own home. You might continue to live as you are presently living, doing what you're doing, and still offer a healing presence of luminosity and compassion to the world around you. You become a co-creator when you align your life with the imprint of mystery, shimmering in the tapestry of your unique life experience. As the poet Rainer Maria Rilke reminds us, 'God speaks to each of us as He makes us':

God speaks to each of us as he makes us,
Then walks with us silently out of the night.
We dimly hear these words;
You sent me out beyond your recall
Go to the limits of your longing.
Embody me. Flare up like flame
In addition, make big shadows I can move in.
Let everything happen to you; beauty and terror.
Just keep going. No feeling is final.
Do not let yourself lose me.
Nearby is the country they call life.[3]

In seeking what the poet calls the 'country they call life', we do not have to have all the answers, or indeed any answers. In fact, the real calling is to embody the challenges and questions of these turbulent times, and to inhabit the space of genuine discernment alongside other sincere seekers.

PRESS PAUSE

Remember, the irrepressible beat of the Divine will never cease to pulsate in the human heart, imprinting new unique callings in every era. There is a promised land hidden deep within the stirrings of the soul.

---

3. Rainer Maria Rilke, *Rilke's Book of Hours: Love Poems to God*, Anita Barrows and Joanna Macy (trans.), NY: Riverhead Books, 1996, p. 88.

Creating Your Trellis

Jot down what is staying with you from this chapter. Where might there be a personal invitation for you?

If you were to 'preach' through your lifestyle, what would this look like?

Take a look around your living space. Does it represent you and your values? Does it honour the Divine living in the temple of your being? Where do you see an invitation for a little seasonal cleaning?

Take some time to identify and list the hopes and dreams that are most important to you in this chapter of your life.

Now identify two avoidant behaviours that keep these dreams out of your reach. These tend to be habits that bring short-term comfort/ease but long-term lack of fulfilment. They keep you in hiding places and tell you to postpone 'showing up' until you are perfect.

Now identify one small step that would bring long-term fulfilment but may cause short-term discomfort. You might, for example, find yourself needing to say something difficult to somebody, perhaps asserting a boundary or claiming your freedom to follow your values, even when it does not fit in with societal demands or with the expectations of those close to you.

CHAPTER FOUR
Called to the Edge

The dangers of life are infinite, and among them is safety.
(GOETHE)

I WAS VERY HAPPY IN MY ROLE AS DIRECTOR OF RETREATS
and programmes in the retreat centre. 'My cup runs over,' I
often sang to myself walking down the corridors. Pat and I
used to often say how fortunate we were, both having secure
permanent jobs that we enjoyed, within short commuting
distance from home. We were unprepared in many ways
for the beat of the new music that emerged from behind
the veil. It emerged softly but clearly, firstly for Pat and
later for me. It was an uncomplicated, simple invitation to
a different way of life, a more soul-aligned rhythm. With it
came a sense that it was time to let go of the familiar. This
brought quite a bit of wrestling on my part. I argued: How
could this be? And, why now? After all, I was happy in my
work. It had meaning and I felt secure, assuring myself that
if I stayed until pension age, sure my barns would be full. I
didn't want to know that I had, like the rose, outgrown my
familiar container, the place where I knew who I was and
what I was about. After spending some time sitting on my
'pity pot', I had to eventually admit that something deep
inside had already chosen to let go.

I didn't have an image of what exactly was ahead; I only
saw an 'edge place', and knew I was being drawn towards it.

I was familiar with this pull towards the edge, as I had gone there many times before. I had left many other securities in the past; however, I thought the pilgrim in me had lost all that restlessness and had finally settled down. But here it was again: the call to the edge, that place where fear and aliveness seem to play off each other. The great Albert Einstein once said, 'Do not grow old, no matter how long you live. Never cease to stand like curious children before the great mystery into which we were born.'

Some friends our age were talking about growing old, planning to retire, and here we were – planning to re-fire. The fiery energies of the spirit seem to have little respect for pension plans; after all, poor old Moses in the Old Testament was eighty when he was called into leadership, and Zechariah, Elizabeth, Anna and Simeon all heard the drumbeat later in life. And, of course, there was Abraham, who at seventy-five thought his life's work was done, until he heard the call from God, 'Go from your country, your people and your father's household to the land I will show you' (Gn 12:1). He was invited to go outside and look at the stars of the night sky, symbols of the promises that Yahweh had for him (Gn 15:5). The night sky visited us also, calling us (or rather dragging us) out of comfortable containers. A night sky star peeked through the window on a late-November evening, and with trembling knees I went out into the dark where I felt drawn to write these lines:

NIGHT SKY MESSENGER
Standing at the edge,
where dusk gives way to dark,
A night sky beckons, with myriad twinkling stars.
A veil lifts, and gentle light pours everywhere,
Sprinkling the world with possibility.
'Leave this land,' the night sky whispers.
A thin place, where sheer delight and terror dance.
'Leave', it beckons, 'for the land that I will show you.'
Barely seeing ahead, through salty waves of grief,
A beating heart that knows it's time,

Called to the Edge

To drink the cup, the crucible of life's uncertainty.
In stepping now from role, to return,
To naked self, and unknown lands,
Lit by silver, night sky messengers.
(MARTINA LEHANE SHEEHAN)

Perhaps at this time, you too sense something in your heart saying, 'It's time.' Maybe there is something deep within, seeking to discover more of this great mystery into which you were born. Perhaps it is now time to let go of something that no longer works, time to lay down a battle that has run its course, time to listen to the night sky messengers inside your heart? In the place where the setting sun gives way to rising moon, where there is a dance of ebb and flow, emptying and filling, dying and rising, there is another voice, a deeper wisdom. Here, you will, most likely, not be asked to create another to-do plan, but perhaps more of a how-to-do-it plan, or simply a to-be plan. You may find yourself asking questions such as these:

How will I live in a way that resonates with a deeper dream, one that contributes to the common good?
How will I create space for what is unlived inside of me?
How will I ... even when those around me share a different world view?

DANGEROUS EDGES

The image of the cliff edge has been nightmare material for me. Maybe it is in remembrance of being on a college trip where we did that rope thing; you know, where you let yourself descend from the cliff, while being held by contraptions that are supposed to keep you safe. I remember how exhilarated the others were as they swooped through the air. I, however, stood paralyzed, frozen, several metres away from the edge. 'Let go, just let go,' they jeered but I could not, would not. Maybe it was trauma from the womb or maybe I fell out of my pram long ago. Whatever it was, I still don't intend to go back to that cliff edge.

There are many metaphorical cliff edges. Those places where things fall apart and we are invited into a deeper trust; where we feel we want to let go, but are unsure we will be held. 'Keep pushing through the fear,' some therapies tell us. I'm not so sure. I think sometimes we need to lean into, soften into the fear and in doing so listen to it compassionately. Paradoxically, it is often when we can 'be with' the vulnerability or the powerlessness that something will shift. And while yes, sometimes the cliff edge is urging us to just let go and leap, pushing ourselves into panic mode never works.

Despite my fear of the edge, I have always been inspired by the idea of 'edge places' in Celtic spirituality. The Celtic monks of old, in frequently going to the edge, were an archetypal image of that inner wrestling between pilgrim and settler. They were usually led to places that were rural, wild and windy, where they built their monasteries. Places like Skellig Michael and Iona.

They would set out in coracles, little boats made of skins that were fixed onto planks of wood. Without oars or rudder, they would set out trusting that they were being led by the Wild Goose, which was the Celtic symbol for the Holy Spirit. (We also felt on many occasions that we were on a bit of a wild goose chase!)

The wild, windy place came into awareness for us not as a far-off destination, but in the simple form of *Ruah*. *Ruah* is the Hebrew word for wind, breath, spirit (sometimes spelled *Ruach*); it is also the name of our house. And so, it was not a geographical journey we were called on, but an inward one, where the cliff edge was more about leaving the comfort zone of security and certainty, and living instead with more unknowns, with the ability to take risks, while trusting in providence. We were drawn to live more simply, travel more lightly, attend to a new pace and daily rhythm and, in doing so, to invite others to share in this way of life for these times.

Letting go of what fits the status quo and allowing ourselves to be led to a life of simplicity is not very exciting to the ego. The ego would much prefer something more extraordinary, a big voyage to save the world and, of course, an applauded return journey. The whisper of the spirit, however, is often low key, not usually attracting any news headlines, yet can radically call us to the edge of our egoic entanglements and so reorient the whole of our life. It tells us to trust the ebb and flow of the heart's tides, to move with greater fluidity, to find a home in the womb of mystery.

LISTENING IN

In a world that is forever shouting at you to push harder, telling you to hurry up, maybe there is another voice gently urging you, not so much to move on but to move in. Of course, this simple 'moving in' doesn't get the same applause, but sometimes it is exactly what we need. We need to 'move in' for a while if we are to hear the promptings of divine guidance. Here we usually only get to see the next right step to take, and then another step. Just as the satnav in the car gives one clear instruction at a time, so it is with your internal satnav. This inner soul guidance is a reliable and purposeful force, navigating you step by step from within.

Setting the intention to serve the energy of soul moves us beyond a life manoeuvred and strategised to merely ensure we don't stand on any sleeping dragons. It is much different to a life driven by compulsions and fleeting preferences. A life directed by the soul is no longer buffeted about by externals, and depends less on outside props for security or power and more on divine guidance and inner authority. None of this randomly happens, however; it needs our consent. We must set our internal satnav and follow the values, practices and habits that support the journey of the soul. When we reach crossroads or dead ends, we will often be sent somebody to help us with directions.

MENTORS, ELDERS

In the Celtic tradition, soul friends and elders were often sent to give direction at times of transition. They were considered to be gifts from the spirit, sent to help on the journey for a while, sometimes arriving on the path unexpectedly and leaving behind a memorable trail or a question to reflect on. I spoke one day to a wise monk who lived as a hermit in Scotland. He said casually, looking out into the distance, 'You have so much spiritual heritage and richness in Ireland. I often dream that there will one day be a contemporary Gobnait and a Patrick who will create a way of living monastic practices for ordinary seekers.' I looked out into the distance too, doing my best to avoid eye contact, and didn't tell him that I am called after St Gobnait (my baptismal name) and that Pat is called after St Patrick. Why didn't I tell him? A few reasons: firstly, I like to keep my options open, just in case anything pins me down. (Remember how I reacted to the rose being pinned down to the trellis?) Also, Gobnait is associated with bees and Patrick with snakes, and I'm a bit squeamish with both. Besides, I never liked the name Gobnait. In school, when it was written on a report or document I used to hide it. Even still, we sit lightly with the 'Gobnait and Patrick thing'. I suppose we do not want to be setting ourselves up as anything special. However, it is probably true that sometimes our names do give us little interesting insights.

Gobnait was a fifth-century Celtic saint, who was sent through a dream in search of nine white deer. When she arrived in Ballyvourney, West Cork, in the south of Ireland, she saw the nine deer and founded a monastery there. She is considered to be a saint for the sick and her name is Irish for Abigail, which means 'bringer of joy'.

Patrick, which means 'one who frees hostages', was born in 390. He was captured and brought to Ireland, where he lived as a slave under a pagan king, spending long hours in solitude tending sheep. He finally escaped and returned to his homeland. He heard, through a dream, that he must return to Ireland and spread the gospel.

In terms of the meaning of our names, I am not convinced I am like St Gobnait in being a 'bringer of joy'; however, I have frequently heard Pat say under his breath (while doing the wash up) that he feels like St Patrick, 'living like a slave'. Neither of us has any prophetic dreams to report nor is either of us a saint – that's for sure. The type of contemporary monasticism we felt drawn towards is really nothing new or heroic; it is a kind of baptism of the ordinary. It is just one apple falling off a very ancient tree. This ancient wisdom is always seeking new entries into consciousness, and so what we are doing is just one simple expression.

The important call for each of us is to be authentic, rather than extraordinary. The simple life, however, can be the most difficult of all, with its daily challenges around rhythms and commitments. In trying to live authentically, there is a continual need to encounter, with rigorous honesty, our many inner contradictions. This prevents us from becoming tranquilised by some imaginary holiness. While it would be lovely to 'have it all together', we are gradually learning that weakness and sinfulness are no impediments to divine intervention.

MENTORS IN THE PUB

We were blessed with the encouragement of an *Anam Cara*, the well-known and well-loved author, the late Fr Daniel J. O'Leary, a dear friend, who helped to birth the project. He spent hours trawling through the ideas we had scribbled on bits of paper and we spent a long evening and night drinking Guinness in a pub in Kerry working out the vision. Suddenly, sitting up straight on his chair, with that adorable glint in his eyes, he said, 'Get me another ham sandwich and a pint, and I'll tell ye what I think.' After a bite and a sip he said emphatically, 'Ye must do this, the future cannot just depend on "priesteens" like myself! Life is an adventure and it is short.' These words were indeed poignant as he was diagnosed with a terminal illness soon afterwards and departed from this life within the year. 'Ye must do this' stayed with us. (*We hope you're still with us on that journey, Daniel.*)

MAD MONKS

On more than one occasion, we felt (and still feel) a little mad, but maybe madness is a necessary ingredient in creating anything new. Often we associate hermits, mystics and those who live in monasteries with being ascetic, sometimes emaciated with long beards, piercing eyes and white robes; however, there is another type of monasticism emerging, one without a clear blueprint, one which can only be developed through diving in, listening and seeing what emerges. Here there is no marked path, no guidebook, map, or pre-planned strategy. I would love to impress you by pretending we conjured up all of this but, in truth, many people across the globe are also exploring new ways of living more contemplatively and holistically, and are exploring new models of monastic living and intentional communities.

BUILD IT AND THEY WILL COME

Imagination points to all we might yet discover and create.
(ALBERT EINSTEIN)

Each time we were about to give up and pull back into safer waters, a little nudge would come again, as if to say, 'Start off again now, turn your sails to the wind and be led by the breeze of *Ruah*.' We knew we couldn't go it alone and we didn't have any sense of who else was to be on this journey with us. 'Build it and they will come,' Pat kept repeating, quoting the film *Field of Dreams*. We didn't know who 'they' would be but, nevertheless, we decided to build it. In the garden we built a small meditation room and began to adhere to a meditative rhythm of life. Knowing it was a bit unusual to have a meditation/prayer room in our garden, we half-hoped no passers-by would notice. (So much for giving witness!) One day, the postman said, 'You have a fine hen shed built there.' In cowardice, we said nothing; however, a few days later he looked rather quizzically as Pat came out the door of the 'hen shed' with a vacuum cleaner. I guess soon enough the rest of the neighbours were told about the mad couple up the road that vacuum up the chicken poo.

After that incident, we decided not to chicken out any more. We decided to become more transparent and courageous about what we were doing. We committed to inviting anyone who was interested to join us in the intentional holding of a space, adhering to simple daily rhythms of morning and evening meditation/prayer, while adhering to a lifestyle that reverenced creation and the whole web of life. This necessitated quite a bit of decluttering and the stripping away of some excess accumulation until there was less stuff and more space. We knew that the vision would only expand (or contract) in proportion to how much we ourselves would continue to commit to the patterns and practices and take small steps in faith.

The moment we choose, providence comes to meet us, the moment I take a stand, at that very moment providence moves us too. All sorts of things occur to help me that would not have otherwise occurred.[1]

We sat and waited, and waited. Eventually others heard the drumbeat and came, one by one, until we had a community of twelve. (Interesting number, from a gospel perspective.) They wove their way into our hearts, our home and our lives. This growing community shares wisdom and laughter with us, sitting around the table and, surprisingly, there's always enough, even though our pensionable jobs are gone.

When we were all asked to practise social distancing and limit all indoor gatherings, we felt this would be the end of this domestic church; however, the spirit cannot be limited and can move through closed doors, and soon we found ourselves transporting the vision of Ruah into a virtual community. It is wonderful to be part of the continued sharing with many global gatherings.

Maybe this was what the first Christian communities were like and people are perhaps beginning to replicate

---

1. WH Murray, *The Scottish Himalayan Expedition,* London: Dent and Sons Ltd, 1951, p. 127.

them in a new way, for today. In traditional monasteries people gathered, inspired by a common vision, breathing the language of that era and culture. They supported each other and offered 'soul friendship' to whomever they came in contact with. They lived by a common way of life, known then as a 'rule of life'.

DUSTING OFF THE OLD

Because we are just one ripple, among many, the purpose of my outlining a little of the initiative created in our home is not so that you admire it (although, that is encouraging), but more that you hear something of your own unique drumbeat echoing from the temple of your being. You might begin to sense your own longings to create an alternative way of life for this new era, through the attraction of your own emerging vision. Regardless of age, there is a creative tension in all of us between the pilgrim and the settler. You may find yourself pulling up the pegs of old, familiar tents in order to follow that inner drumbeat. These outworn and sometimes tattered tents are often internal and psychological restrictions, and in rolling them up, you become aware that they can no longer house the height and depth of your expanding consciousness. You may find yourself stretching out and standing more upright, while dusting off whatever veils you from the vision of your magnificent and evolving soul-self.

None of this is about a force of will, or a recreation of the past; rather, it is about the willingness to open to the creative movement of the spirit, that gentle but powerful disturber of mediocrity. She shakes us out of our fear in order to bring us alive, so very alive. Her wild call may lead you to, like Abraham, leave your native country for a new land (Gn 12:1). We might need to disentangle from what might be safe and native to us, so that we can embrace our journey to the new country. The ego likes to cling to what is familiar in all its addictions and resistances; however, it helps to remember that an ego-driven person is actually a frightened person. When our inner world is filled with fear, we lack a sense of internal power and may attempt instead to have 'power over' and control. We have to be very gentle here, because those many rules and regulations, formed in fear, can easily become the habitual native land we revert to. That is why, in letting go of old external scaffoldings, we need to build new internal supports – an unshakeable trellis for the soul. In the next chapter, we will explore this inner trellis in the context of releasing old psychological 'rules' that prevent us from living courageously and intentionally.

PRESS PAUSE

Remember, there is a creative tension in all of us between the pilgrim and the settler. And, so, the call to pull up the pegs of our tents of security can come at any time. The important call for each of us is to be authentic, rather than extraordinary.

Creating Your Trellis

Jot down what is staying with you from this chapter. Where might there be a personal invitation for you?

Reflect on your name and its origins. Say your name aloud. What invitation might it carry?

Begin a dialogue between the settler and the pilgrim; the part that wants safety and certainty, and the part that wants growth and newness.

Identify how you may have 'pitched your tent' in a place that keeps you in the comfort zone. While it may be keeping you safe, it could also be preventing you from growing and expanding. Consider, therefore, how you might take one small challenging step towards some creative edge at this time? (This step must not push you to the panic zone, but keep you in the self-care zone.)

Now, see what might be another small step, one that is true to you and honours your need for creativity, purpose and balance.

CHAPTER FIVE
Out with the Old: Re-wiring and Re-firing

'JUST PICKING UP SOME PAINT FOR A MAKEOVER,' SAID THE lady next to me in the queue in the hardware shop. 'Oh how exciting,' I said as I looked into her trolley, full of paint cans. 'What colours are here?' 'Grey,' she said, in a rather flat voice, 'I'm doing the whole house grey. I don't actually like grey myself, but the painter said it's all in, so I have to do grey.' She proceeded to place about fifty shades of grey paint on the counter. After paying for them, she looked back briefly as I placed my own few cans on the counter – vibrant blue, deep mustard, soft sage and a bit of pink. 'For the chairs,' I explained. She looked at me with a rather grey expression.

'It's all in, so I have to do grey.' Her words stayed with me. I suppose we can all identify with something here because, while grey can indeed be a classy colour for decor and there is nothing wrong with following fashion and trends, excessive blending-in and watching over our shoulder to see who we are impressing or who is disapproving, leads to a rather grey life. Whether we find ourselves following every fad, led by the world of advertising, or every popular public opinion, we can easily become devoid of colour and lose our own unique way of being in the world. Wouldn't it be better to enjoy whatever is 'in' without making it a rule that enslaves us?

Before we look at the concept of a rule of life, we will look at some of the rules we may already be following;

some old introjected rules that perhaps were never of our own choosing but continue to automate our lives and limit our choices.

INTERNAL RULES

I continually failed to get into a file on the computer one morning, and then I spotted a sentence in the lower left corner that read, 'Old scripts still running.' It stayed with me all day. Old scripts still running can sabotage a lot of our best intentions. Instead of forging ahead, perhaps we need to take a look to see what old, preprogrammed rules might still be running, from our upbringing or from introjected old programmes. We might need to delete some of them, especially if they are related to old messages of unworthiness. These beliefs can drive us to excessively depend on titles, roles, status and other compensations for our perceived lack. No matter how much we compensate with declarative statements about our achievements and performances, we can continue to be held back by old scripts running in the subconscious. No matter how many accolades we have garnered, nothing will ever be enough until we ourselves accept that we are enough.

Whatever gets stored in our memory creates automatic patterns. So, for example, if you have a belief system stored away that says *I must blend in* or *I must not speak out because people must like me and I must not be seen to be different*, you will continue, on autopilot, to act and react out of that 'rule'. There are many outworn rules with a genesis in the past that may be still pulling the strings in our present-day lives. We all make unconscious choices, many of which are made at a young age, often based on fear. Shame and self-sabotage are particularly toxic scripts. They tend to attack the core of the innocent soul. If, for example, you were shamed as a child for taking some spontaneous risk or simply for appearing vulnerable, you would most likely have made an unconscious rule to never trust again, or to never appear vulnerable, or to avoid showing weakness or failure (or maybe even to avoid success, or happiness). These unconscious rules can get wired into our identity and, so, can continue to subtly work against our best intentions and goals. We sometimes even carry life-diminishing scripts that have been passed from one generation to the next. All of these can hold us back – a bit like driving a car while continually looking at the rear-view mirror.

RENEWING THE MIND

Do not be conformed to this world, but be transformed by the renewing of your minds. (RM 12:2)

Many who come for spiritual direction and counselling speak of having restrictive internal rules. One lady said that all her life she had followed the rule that she must stay in the background and not speak out. She admitted that, in following this rule, she often held a subtle resentment towards those who allow themselves to speak out and allow themselves to be seen and to let their gifts shine in the world. She gradually discovered that by dismantling this unhelpful introjected belief, she could remove the bushel blocking her light and so create a new conscious permission in alignment with her values. She called this her new rule of life, a trellis for her soul.

Another lady said she was exhausted from striving for social conformity, trying to get everyone's approval. She discovered she was unconsciously following an old rule of life based on the 'disease to please'.

'I'm weary from following these internal, rigid rules where there is no room for failure, where I have to be expert at everything.' These were the words of an elderly man I spoke with recently. He said that all of his life he only allowed himself to engage in the 'tried and tested', in what was guaranteed to succeed and he never 'let an unexamined word flow from his mouth'. Long ago he had vowed he would protect himself with excessive caution and self-reliance. Now, in sheer exhaustion, he recognised that he had created what he described as 'vows' to protect him. These were formed unconsciously after he endured a series of losses and betrayals in early childhood. After exploring them a little deeper, he straightened up and with a sudden broad smile said, 'I want to learn to let go of these unhelpful vows, and learn to live before I die.'

SLEEPWALKING

By our nature, most of us tend to follow the path of least resistance. We find ourselves sleepwalking down well-worn pathways. Sometimes old rules repress parts of the psyche, creating a disharmony within us. Rules that keep us in cognitive busyness and other avoidances can cause a kind of dissociation. This is sometimes called 'somaticizing' (*soma* is Latin for 'body'). Anything repressed gets stored in the body, where it can continue to subtly drain our energy. There are four main ways we dissociate: numbing out; distraction; excessive thinking; self-sabotage behaviours. We usually employ these diversionary tactics to get away from uncomfortable inner feelings, such as shame, grief and vulnerability. If, for example, you have a rule that says, *I must never show weakness,* you will then numb/turn away from that part of yourself, resulting in no longer being 'fully there'. At a very young age, I made a promise not to ask for anything and not to ever cry. I made this vow because I knew it would be one less burden in a home where sickness and pain dominated. It was a dangerous vow and took a lifetime to reverse.

We might create a subtle rule that serves to mask our inferiority. We often do this by competing and making sure we are 'better' than everyone else. It is as if we are saying, *If I cannot feel as good as you, I'll make myself better than you.* Inferiority is just the other side of superiority, causing the same kind of chronic soul pain.

REPETITION

We usually form reactions from whatever is stored in our memory. We endorse old beliefs such as: *this is what I'm good at/not good at; this is how people should/shouldn't be; this is safe/unsafe.* This continuous automatic processing can dull your capacity to be fully present to your experience in the here and now. The more a belief or rule is repeated, the stronger and denser that go-to habit becomes until it forms what is called a neurological pathway. The earlier these automatic pathways develop, the more they affect the structure of the developing brain. Consequently, we often start avoiding situations that might threaten these old endorsed pathways with all their unhelpful governing rules. This tends to dull our ability to hear and experience any new information. Neuroscientist, Daniel Siegel, calls this 'top down' brain processing.

While these rules may be imprisoning, they can subtly become normalised, taking up residence in the psyche, where they become part of our character structure. We can become so used to these limitations that we learn to just 'put up with them'. Because of this adaptation, deep resistance can set in, which makes any change quite difficult.

Internal pressures, such as, *I should do everything perfectly* or *I should prove my worth* or *I must not let my vulnerability be seen,* can become automatic rules that we blindly obey. They can become moral codes which hide under the guise of 'holiness'.

Nearly thirty years ago, I was searching for a spiritual director. In my innocence, I decided to look for the holiest one I could find. I was recommended an elderly monk, whom I was told was indeed very holy. I went along, full of zeal, and started to tell him about all my aspirations to become more spiritual and devotional, asking him to give me a list of what I should and shouldn't do: Should I fast? Should I say more prayers? Should I give up this, and that? All the while, his eyes were twinkling. I waited, my pen pointed towards my notebook, ready to write his wise, prescriptive advice. He slowly drew a breath and said, 'Martina, you seem to have a lot of shoulds. My advice, therefore, is "shit on should".' Needless to say, I was horrified, aghast, and vowed I would never again go back to this 'holy' monk; however, to this day, I have not forgotten his advice, especially when I'm listing off 'should haves' and 'shouldn't haves'.

The good news is that old automatic rules and reactive patterns can be altered. Deadening and life-draining habits can be weakened and new healthy ones can be strengthened. The habitual fight/flight/freeze response can be transformed to a more rest-and-digest way of being. Integrating new practices such as gratitude, stillness, self-compassion and the sending of blessings helps us to form new healthy neural trails.

OLD HABITS DIE HARD

Neurons are cells in the nervous system that transmit information through signals known as neurotransmitters. Pathways are created through the repetitive carrying of messages between neurons. Anything repeated over time results in a thickening of the neural pathway that gets wired into our neurology. 'Those who pray together, stay together,' we were told growing up. For some, this can be a rather depressing prospect. Equally depressing can be the phrase, 'The neurons that fire together, wire together.' This is only depressing, however, if we are repeating unhelpful, outdated messages. It is exciting to know that neuroscience now demonstrates that we can create new neural pathways. The brain can repair itself through the weakening of old paths and the forming of new ones (neuroplasticity). Cultivating new pathways through repetition and discipline is like strengthening unused muscles; it takes dedicated and regular practice. Eventually, our new habits and actions become embedded and gradually become our new 'normal'.

WE BECOME WHAT WE PRACTISE
Your beliefs become your thoughts,
Your thoughts become your words,
Your words become your actions,
Your actions become your habits,
Your habits become your values,
Your values become your destiny.
(MAHATMA GANDHI)

There are many ways that we can change neural trails and create new neural pathways but the two most effective ways are meditation (or contemplative prayer), and intentionally changing small habits and actions:

- ◆ In meditation/contemplative prayer, the prefrontal cortex is activated. This allows us to witness, while not engaging in, passing thought patterns. When we mindfully notice, rather than continually 'feed', every passing thought, the incessant stream of mental activity begins to weaken. In this way, gradually, new pathways can be formed, based on attentiveness, stillness and empathy.

- ◆ The second way we can interrupt old neural wiring is by creating new everyday small actions. When we become aware that certain habits have become embedded in our neurology, we can begin to create new regular habits and make small choices each day to weaken these old pathways and strengthen new ones. We can, for example, choose to see new dimensions in those we live or work with. We can seek out new information about people and situations rather than reacting and endorsing what we already think we know about them. We could ask new questions, such as: Where is the gift in this encounter? What is the invitation here? What new information is here? All of this creates cognitive flexibility that transforms old fixed neurological trails.

While old unconscious habits can foster staleness in our way of seeing, we can begin with small, simple changes that expand our range of options. It can be as simple as walking a different route to the shops and intentionally noticing new things along the way. We can gradually let go of some old habits and routines that have kept us shut down and numbed for many years. A commitment to this gradual cognitive expansion can be part of a newly introduced rule of life, a trellis for the soul.

NEW WINE, NEW WINESKINS

We can have many wonderful experiences, but if they land onto old belief systems, we will miss their meaning and their potential to transform us. You will know it is time for the new when what once protected you is now stifling. In the Gospel of Matthew, Jesus says that in order to hold the new wine, we need new wineskins (9:14-17) – no point in pouring something new into old containers. The new wine, the new life will stretch the rules of the old comfort zone. When this happens, we discover some old, familiar life-horizon becomes outgrown, beckoning that it is time for letting go. When we begin to realise that some of the old rules we absorbed have now become too small for us, we will need to discern new ways of respecting our inner guidance.

Don't risk exposure; keep your cards close to your chest; don't put yourself out there was the old rule I introjected in early life. Even now as I write this book, a little sneaky inner voice pops in and tells me to avoid any self-revelation or exposure, saying, 'At least wait until you've got it all together.' In my hometown of Cork in the south of Ireland, we have an expression when we know something will not work. We say, 'Good luck with that one, girl!'

We have to challenge many of our old internal rules, because they can lead to us becoming over cautious and cynical of others who take risks. I consider cynicism to be the least creative option for living; in fact, it is probably one of the greatest sins against life. To hide safely and cynically while sitting on the fence asks nothing of us. It invites no vulnerability and no growth. In replacing this rule, we must, again and again, choose to get off the fence and risk the uncertainty of being a player on the playground of life. While you can be jeered and laughed at on that playground, you can also be supported and championed. Getting off the fence and getting into your life is the only way you can be fully alive.

A SOLID CENTRE

We are in an ever-changing world; our bodies age, people change, spring surrenders to summer and autumn gives way to winter. No matter how desperately we try to hold onto a season, a place, person or possession, everything is in a state of constant flux and change. We all need, therefore, some kind of inner anchor, a place that continues to endure as each season and situation slips away, a steadfast place we can call home.

No matter how many places of belonging the world offers us, we end up feeling homeless if we do not belong to ourselves. If, for example, I am habitually people-pleasing, I need to become aware that by continually obeying your rules and selling out on my own, I will eventually become resentful of you. When we live our lives by trying to fit in with everyone else's rules, we carry a lurking fear that at any moment, we might be kicked out of the universe. Expecting others to grant us our worthiness to belong will never satisfy; this is something we must learn to grant for ourselves. We can do this not by perfecting ourselves but through 'showing up' with both our gifts and our imperfections.

We need to sift through and decide which rules we want to retain and which we want to let go. We will need to discern where we need to reach out and where we need to draw back. Throughout your life, though you may get seduced by many conditional promises based on earning and proving, you can still find a way of returning to a seat of wisdom at the centre of your being. In the account of Christ in the desert, we hear that he was offered many false promises, but he returned again and again to his inner guidance, his rule of life, the divine home in the depths of his being. Similarly, in the desert of our hearts, we too have a divine home, but we need deliberate pauses and daily rhythms to stay connected to it. In the next chapter, we will explore how to return to that centre, to the ground of our being. We will learn how to introduce new habits and permissions in order to nourish the soulful life.

PRESS PAUSE

Remember, by dismantling unhelpful introjected rules you can create a new conscious rule of life, which, when placed in alignment with your values, increases states of joy and contentment.

Creating Your Trellis

Jot down what is staying with you from this chapter. Where might there be a personal invitation for you?

Maybe, like the rose, there is a container you have outgrown. What restrictive rules keep this tight container in place? Where did these rules come from?

We tell ourselves stories about our limitations and rules and we then look for evidence to endorse them. Finish this sentence: The story I often tell myself is ...

Now write out a few of the rules within that story:

I must not ...
It's not okay to be seen ...
I shouldn't ever ...

How does each of these internal pressures feel in the body? In what ways do you tend to justify these old rules and narratives?

Are there any you can begin to discard?

Visualise yourself beginning to move more freely, as if you are stretching your roots deep and wide into the soil of your being, and waving your branches into the welcoming fresh air.

CHAPTER SIX
Creating the Trellis

If today, like every other day,
you wake up frightened and empty.
Don't open the door to the study and begin reading.
Take down the dulcimer.
Let the beauty we love be what we do.
(RUMI)

WHAT IS THE 'BEAUTY YOU LOVE' AND WHAT WOULD IT BE like if your life revolved more around it? Ask yourself this question: What makes my heart sing? Give this plenty of time so that the response can unfold gradually. Be honest here: if you weren't worrying about what others thought of you, what would you be doing differently? Much of what keeps us busy fails to bring beauty or meaning into our lives, and sometimes can leave us tragically numbed.

At the beginning of the Covid-19 pandemic lockdown, many people said to Pat and I, 'You will be fierce busy now.' They were referring to counselling practices being impacted by the forecasted rise in mental health difficulties. Surprisingly, we were not. One of my clients said she expected to be 'climbing the walls' without her usual distractions, like shopping expeditions for designer gear; however, in the slower pace, she discovered that all of these distractions were not the beauty for which her soul truly longed. To her surprise, she actually became quite reluctant to return to her former way of life with all its glitter and glitz.

Interestingly, it was when restrictions started to lift that we became 'fierce busy' in counselling. I think this was because, deep down, people didn't want to return to a way of life that drowned out the desire to live the beauty we love. We now know that life has changed and we must dive deep in discerning that which endures when things fall apart at the seams. When my 2020 diary fell apart, I wrote these few lines:

MY 2020 DIARY
Checking and re-checking my 2020 diary,
Flicking back to read the plans,
All made in springtime's first unfolding.
To-do lists hammered onto pristine page.
Hours and days beaten into servitude,
designed to stock my barns til harvest time.
I check, re-check, but pages now lay fallow,
and life itself
postponed til harvest time.

No marked-out times or hours
to glue these days together.
Unhinged, I wander in this 2020 desert.
My busyness, the mantle that I've woven,
hangs idle in the hallway.
While I'm busy going nowhere,
being no one, and wondering
How ever will I fill this empty time?

How ever will I fill it?
I turn to ask the daisies,
But they don't seem to grasp the question.
They giggle, just a little,
so I ask a dandelion instead.
How ever will I fill these empty days?
I ask the birds,

76

who do not spin or weave.
And I spin all the time, so how will I get through?
I'll ask the wildflower dressed in splendour,
basking in the sun.
She winks and twirls and shakes,
so I stay a little while.
And then I know what I will do:
I'll make a business plan, a strategy.

So here it is:
Today, I'll learn to sway a little with the wildflowers
and allow the birds to teach me how to chant.
Then I'll lie down in the grass, and belly breathe,
Tutored by my dog, a wiser soul than I.

I'll eat breakfast late at night, and dinner anytime.
I'll watch the sun set in my soul,
and wait for Sister Moon to rise.
And it will be enough. We all will be enough.
Sure won't we all be strolling gardens in eternity,
arm in arm, swaying with the wildflowers
and lying in Heaven's meadow,
drinking cups of wonder
until filled to overflowing.

So, in the meantime, let's sit lightly with the diary.
Take it from the shelf,
and now and then just sketch a dream,
and make a plan or two.
But do it all in pencil, in the 2020 diary.
(MARTINA LEHANE SHEEHAN)

SPACE AND STRUCTURE

Sometimes, those who habitually go with the flow might discover they need to create structure, while those who are over-structured will need to allow more flow – through creating some unplanned, open spaces. Where are you in this? Do you ever find yourself dreaming about endless, unstructured free time, with the promise of catching up on those books you never got time to read, and the coffee with friends that hasn't happened in ages? Bliss. Doesn't the idea of all that free time hold great promise? However, we often discover that we humans don't handle long spans of time very well. We seem to need a combination of open spaces and gentle structure to create a rhythm to our days and our lives. Like the rose, we need a trellis, not for the sake of rigidity, but as a tool to support our growth.

Some of those who completed the *Trellis for the Soul* transformational programme agreed to share a few of their ideas. All agreed that concepts and ideas have to be turned into intentions and actions. In our online programme, Anne created a way of life that reduced busyness and chose to put love, gratitude and kindness at the centre. Staying close to nature and honouring the seasons internally as well as externally became more important to her. Mary said, 'The rule of life puts what matters most at the centre ... to help me on the path I need to create a solid, but flexible structure.' (She wrote it in chalk on a blackboard so it could be adapted over time.) Decluttering, journaling and stillness were priorities for her. One of the commitments that resonated for Peggy was the practice of centering prayer, which we explore in chapter fifteen. She also committed to reclaiming 'Sabbath' and attending to creation more intentionally. Martha, on writing her commitments, divided them into daily, weekly and monthly practices. These included writing from gratitude each night, supporting local community events, conscious shopping and daily commitment to recycling. Jean also emphasised daily commitments and said she would take regular 'prayer pauses' throughout the day, as well as integrating the habit of sending blessings. She also made a commitment to go on pilgrimages (inner ones as well as visits to holy wells). Geraldine became more aware of how she nourishes her soul. She made a commitment to reduce her exposure to the graphic reporting of incidents in news bulletins and to violence, particularly by being discerning in her choices of films and television. She made a commitment to increase exposure to things of beauty like art, music and nature. She also felt drawn to live more simply and to care for the earth. Jane said that when creating her trellis she would remember the advice of the desert dwellers long ago: 'Take the cell with you, it will hold you and teach you what you need to know.' 'The cell' for Jane was an inner at-home-ness, an inner stillness when life became overwhelming.

As I write this book I keep an eye on the trellised rose. Today she looks a little more wild and free, sharing her colour with the world. She tells me that she is happy to have something to lean against. It supports her, yet doesn't restrict her natural unfolding. The trellis, being made up of interweaving horizontal and vertical lines, helps the rose to grow in the direction of the sun.

A trellis for the soul can provide us with something to lean against on days we feel directionless, while aligning us with practices that keep us growing towards the light. For me, reading a poem each day, taking time for journaling and reflecting on a few lines of scripture are like daily vitamins for my soul and, so, are part of the scaffolding of my spiritual life. However, one of my non-negotiable practices is the regular creating of space for reflection in the early morning. This is where I set my compass to be open to the gift of the twenty-four hours stretching out before me. Without this early-morning ritual on my trellis, the cosmic pain of the world would overwhelm and topple me. As the poet Rumi says, 'What nine months of attention does for an embryo, forty early mornings will do for your gradually growing wholeness.'

You might personally have no attraction to early mornings, but there are other practices and daily patterns that would support you in your gradually growing wholeness.

RULE OF LIFE
This is what the Lord says, 'stand at the crossroads, and look, and ask for the ancient paths, where the good way is, and walk in it.' (JER 6:16)

As we mentioned already, the idea of a rule of life came from the monastic tradition and today, in secular circles, might be referred to simply as a lifestyle choice. The English word 'rule' is derived from the Latin *regula*, meaning 'to regulate' and also meaning 'pattern'. This suggests that a rule of life has something to do with regulating and having a pattern in our lives. It refers to something deeper than just a list of rules, or things to do or not do. In fact, a rule of life is not a to-do list at all; it is more a to-be and to-become list.

In contrast to imposed moral codes, a rule of life, does not stop the flow of life. It is not something that represses life, but something which supports life. It can give direction to our inner energies and can animate our life force. It doesn't always change circumstances but it changes our relationship to them.

The watering can in the garden has a nozzle in the spout that allows the water to creatively spray forth, lightly touching the plants. Without this nozzle, the water just cascades out in an undirected way. Likewise for us; in order to go with the flow, we need something that offers a gentle direction to help us balance our many daily commitments. This 'something' cannot be another pressure to add to an already busy life, nor is it something created by our idealised self with all its impossible standards and perfectionism. While there can be a buzz in raising the bar to unattainable heights, in the long term this becomes only a breeding ground for frustration. Instead, a rule of life – a trellis for the soul – can offer new steady challenges and permissions, while softening the hard edges of our ego demands. Sometimes it reminds us to step back, to choose what is most important and to then automate our lives based on our deeper values. In this way, we will find ourselves less compulsive in trying to respond to everything and everyone. Instead, whenever we find ourselves bombarded with the needs of the world, rather than feeling powerless and overwhelmed, we will pause to ask ourselves, 'How can I authentically respond to this situation?'

Creating a trellis can be a simple but powerful way to help you visualise all the important areas of your life. This visual representation can help you to understand which areas are flourishing, and which are languishing and in need of attention. We might discover some neglect in one of these areas: relationships, finances, health, hobbies, career/mission, self-care, prayer, community or contribution.

While modern culture suggests you set goals to strive for more – become more assertive, more successful, more fit, more productive – rarely does it suggest we set a goal to become more generous, more hospitable or more kind. Interestingly, recent research in the studies of happiness suggests that values such as contribution and service are integral and necessary ingredients for well-being. Most importantly, instead of craving more, we do much more for our well-being by practising a sense of abundance; having a sense of enough.

SO, WHEN IS ENOUGH, REALLY ENOUGH?

There was a time when I felt as if I never had enough. This often caused me to act quite ungenerously towards myself. On one occasion, thirty-five years ago, a group of us were going to the Rose of Tralee Festival. On the day before, I decided to withdraw my name, calculating how much I would save by not going. I put away the saved money in an envelope and put it carefully into a drawer at work. That very day, the money was stolen from the drawer. It was never found and I concluded a member of the public had spotted me putting it there and took advantage. Later that evening, lamenting how I could have been with my friends enjoying myself, I vowed to never allow a sense of scarcity to dominate again. Now, I sometimes have a full drawer, other times an empty one, but somehow I always feel rich. I feel rich in the supports I have, the kindness around me, rich in my appreciation of opportunities, rich that I have shelter and food, that I can get out of bed each morning, rich that I have green trees outside the window, and so much more. A prosperous heart has really very little to do with a bank balance because a sense of enough primarily comes from within.

ALIGNING WITH OUR VALUES

'Wait till you hear this, you won't believe it,' she whispered. I leaned in to join the group, all listening to a bit of juicy gossip over a glass of wine. A cosy little huddle began to form between us, with all the warm, fuzzy feeling that goes with being on the inside of a secret. 'Sure, it's a harmless habit,' I convinced myself, as I began to satisfy that old embedded hedonistic part of the brain that seeks to be part of the tribe.

Suddenly, the warm, fuzzy feeling was replaced with a tight, restrictive sensation around my heart. I realised that the poison was passing through me while I was 'innocently' spreading it around. With this realisation came a sudden awareness that hurting another is also hurting myself because we are all one. The gossip didn't feel as juicy now, and I didn't want to feed this destructive habit any more. I interrupted the huddle and said, 'If you don't mind, I'd rather not continue with this.' My withdrawal wasn't greatly received, but despite the short-term discomfort of feeling unpopular, this choice to stay true to a deeper set of values brought a long-lasting feeling of relief and peace. This experience imprinted itself in my consciousness so strongly that Pat and I decided to make a commitment to create a 'zero gossip tolerance' in our home. Now whenever we find ourselves engaging in something negative (such as judging, gossiping or criticising), we remind one another of the commitment we have made. Over time, we have noticed that any short-term buzz does not equal the long-term peace that comes with staying true to this chosen value. Scripture advises, 'Keep your tongue free from evil, and your lips free from speaking deceit. Depart from evil, and do good; seek peace, and pursue it' (Ps 34:13–15).

It helps to remember that whenever we engage in negativity, we don't just contaminate the energy around us; we also activate a part of the brain, known as the right prefrontal cortex, that contributes to our own low mood. However, whenever we replace these habits with uplifting practices such as compassion, empathy and kindness, we access higher parts of the brain where happiness lies (the left prefrontal cortex). So, maybe we need to remember that we are building new happy brains each time we cultivate wholesome attitudes and conversations. We can make a choice to interrupt the downward spiral, which often begins innocently with something like, 'Did you hear about ...'

Values need to be freely chosen and respectful of our personalities, our resources and the stage of life we are in. They can act as an internal barometer that guides us towards flourishing rather than floundering or merely meandering along according to the expectations of others. When we choose to follow our values, those closest to us may not always understand and might, therefore, not be in accord with our choices. Remember that when Jesus had made up his mind to embrace the divine plan of his difficult destiny, his best friend, Peter, tried to stop him, saying, 'This must not happen to you' (Mt 16:22). Similarly, out of genuine concern our friends and family may try to dissuade us from following the route we know we need to follow. In such times, we will need to consult, and remain resolute in and aligned with, the values we have chosen as part of our trellis for the soul. Filling in these few statements might offer hints about where your values lie:

I'm firing on all cylinders when ...
The people I admire, who follow their passion, are ...
I feel drained, distracted and listless when ...
The work that brings meaning to me is ...
I feel a sense of inner peace when ...
When I sell out on my values, I feel ...
When I do not fear other people's opinions, I am ...

A trellis for the soul needs to be built on small choices and practices that point in the direction of your values, and not just based on short-term comfort or illusory relief. When, for example, you find yourself cancelling out, procrastinating or avoiding something challenging, there can be short-term relief, but later you will most likely feel disappointed in yourself. On such occasions, you can ask:

What value am I moving away from by this avoidance/distraction? What value do I need to move towards? It might, in such situations, help to remember the benefit of enduring short-term pain for long-term gain. Remember, whenever you are aligned with one of your values, even if it is temporarily uncomfortable, you will, at a deeper level, experience a sense of congruence and aliveness.

OUR BETTER ANGELS

The founding father of psychoanalysis, Sigmund Freud (1856–1939), who is often considered to be a bit pessimistic, surprisingly, on one occasion, admits that we are here 'to serve our nature's better angels'. Even though he talks much about what he called the 'id impulse' (the part of the human mind that only wants pleasure and an easy life), he says we are meant to reach our potential, and also to move to a world beyond ourselves. The hedonic part of us can keep us stuck in a very small range of options: on the path of least resistance and instant gratification. If we base our lives on acquiring fleeting pleasures or possessions, we will, because of this 'hedonic adaptation', revert to spiritual bankruptcy and a fairly flat existence. However, something in us – guided by our better angels – knows there is another way. Rather than assigning away responsibility, allowing others to be the architects of your life, you can access that inbuilt wisdom that knows you are made for a more magnificent, higher, deeper purpose.

ACROSS TRADITIONS

Saint Benedict (480–547), who is considered to be the founder of Western monasticism, crafted a rule of life to help the monks intentionally place their spiritual values at the centre. He encouraged a balanced lifestyle and advised they not get too attached to passing things and concerns, but that they remind themselves each day that everything is transitory. Moderation was encouraged, and in order to achieve this St Benedict suggested a continual practice of deep listening 'with the ear of the heart'.

The language of his rule was breathing the culture of that era, yet it is still relevant for today. 'Your way of acting should be different from the world's way,' states the Rule of St Benedict (4:20). It is important that we not interpret his rule incorrectly. When St Benedict suggests that we should be 'different from the world', the ego might latch onto this, creating a false mysticism, a kind of 'ascetic withdrawal' from the messy everyday life. The true meaning of being 'different from the world' is choosing values and loosening some of those societal attachments that can enslave us. It asks us to make personal choices based on conscience when creating a more intentional way of life. Saint Benedict is known for asking the question, 'Is there anyone here who yearns for life and desires to see good days?' A rule of life is, therefore, for those of us who yearn for life.

All faith traditions have a rule of life. The Vinaya, which is the regularising framework of Buddhist monasticism is sometimes synthesised into ten precepts or moral codes. This is based on the importance of developing character traits on the path to enlightenment. All faith traditions have something about non-violence, the sacredness of all of life, loving kindness in speech, intention and an encouraged balance between contemplation and action, service and hospitality.

Some of the ancient wording in a lot of these codes for behaviour can, out of context, seem rigid and be off-putting. However, this is more about a reflection of the era and how it is breathing the language of that time. Whether reading rules from Islamic teachings or studying an ancient text from the Buddhist Vinaya or Christian monasticism, we need to strip some of the archaic language and old systemic encrustations and interpret it through the lens of our modern world. So, while we can be enriched by tradition, our choices need to be in consultation with what is deepest within. We are nowadays fortunate to be able to integrate the ancient wisdom with evolved understandings in theology, psychology and science.

INTERPRETING FOR TODAY

A contemporary rule of life would look different from traditional ones. It would integrate some new developments in our understanding of the universe, and in the theology of creation. Theologian Ilia Delio tells us, 'The whole Creation, beginning with the Big Bang, is incarnation. Evolution is the process of unfolding life; from matter to spirit ... the God of evolution is the God of adventure, a God who loves to do new things, and is always new. We are invited to this adventure of love to find our freedom in love, and to love without measure.'[1] This 'adventure of love' is always evolving and maturing in each of us.

In the past, I was attracted to and explored living the life of an enclosed contemplative. I suppose this never quite left. It continued to stalk my soul but over time has changed direction. Over the years, it sought a new entry into my consciousness, and I grew increasingly interested in how to apply traditional foundational essentials to everyday contemporary life.

MONASTERY OF THE SOUL

Today we often feel buffeted about between fundamental extremes and a sort of deleting of any reference to the mystery underpinning our lives. When the tight container of institutionalism begins to crack, the life of the spirit can burst forth in all sorts of wild, wonderful directions. This has to happen because only dead things can remain static and unchanging. All this wildness needs some support, otherwise we are likely to throw out the plant with the pot. New growth is always tender and often needs a support, or a trellis, and so it is with us. We require, according to author, Mary Lou Kownacki, OSB, 'a lifestyle, which is centred on the "necessary" thing, an attentiveness to God developed through a certain rhythm, a certain sense of daily priorities which must not degenerate into the fixtures of custom as an end in itself'.[2] Spiritual transformation is not just a set

---

1. Ilia Delio, *The Emergent Christ*, NY: Orbis Books, 2011, pp. 153, 156.
2. Mary Lou Kownacki, OSB, *Peace is our Calling*, PA: Benet Press, 1981, p. 6.

of beliefs in the head; it is not so much about concepts and ideas, but a way of living with intention, rhythm and practice.

WRITTEN IN YOUR HEART

We are all hardwired to evolve. It is an innate creative force that seems to be coded into all of creation and written into our hearts: 'I will put my law within them, and I will write it on their hearts' (Jer 31:33). Psychologist, Carl Jung tells us, 'To the extent that a man is untrue to the law of his being and does not rise to personality, he has failed to realise his life's meaning. Fortunately, in her kindness and patience, nature never puts the fatal question as to the meaning of their lives into the mouths of most people. And where no one asks, no one needs answer.'[3] If we are 'untrue to the law of our being', we cannot flourish.

Without an inwardly directed intention or barometer to guide us, distractions and disturbances will ruffle our equilibrium. We will need to dig deep into the soil of our being to discover and name our intention, because the ego is cunning and will give us a different picture from the one that will truly make our heart sing. The ego will tell us to satisfy the status quo, to impress others, to never rock the boat, but we end up exiled from our own truth.

Saint Benedict, in his rule of life, uses the image of a ladder, which he says one must climb in humility, 'That ladder must be raised up by our mounting actions; that ladder which appeared to Jacob in the dream and on which were shown to him angels coming down and going up.'[4] None of the participants on our *Trellis for the Soul* transformational programme have reported meeting any angels on the way but they certainly did meet themselves.

A gentle trellis can help us attune to what is already written in our hearts. It provides us with a decision-making

3. Carl Jung, quoted in John Welch, *Spiritual Pilgrims*, NJ: Paulist Press, 1982, p. 31.
4. Beverly Lanzetta, *The Monk Within: Embracing a Sacred Way of Life*, Sebastopol, CA: Blue Sapphire Books, 2018, p. 341.

framework that helps us to be clear about who we are and where we are going. We are, consequently, thrown off course less easily and less frequently.

EVERY YES, REQUIRES A NO

Pat and I explored what rhythms would best suit a way of life where we could be available and flexible enough to respond to the call of an unfolding vision. Working in the area of counselling and retreats, and now also cultivating a spirit of community, meant we couldn't just tick-box our work. We needed space for reflection; otherwise we would be only skimming the surface in our interactions, unable to be fully present to others. We discovered that saying *yes* to one thing necessitated saying *no* to something else. We chose, therefore, to say yes to practices, such as:

- A simpler lifestyle and a decluttering of excess.
- A daily practice of meditation/contemplation based on monastic practices of centering prayer and Lectio Divina.
- Commitment to caring for the earth.
- A more healthy balance of service, contribution, hospitality and outreach.
- A weekly 'Sabbath Space': time to allow the soul to lie fallow, while also writing a weekly Sabbath reflection for our growing online community.

These are just a few of the commitments we chose and are a work in progress. The most important dimension is the sharing and support of a growing community. Of course, we rise and fall continually and can never truly say that we've got it; however, in as much as we fall off the wagon, there is a deep fulfilment in seeking to live and share these lifestyle habits and practices.

PRACTICES AND PATTERNS

Consider how your own trellis could be built with some regular, strengthening practices, which will help you to stay aligned to your core values. Remember, this is a much more solid way of living than depending on moods and reactions (which are usually transitory and often based on our emotional temperatures on any given day). When you have an inner anchor, the world of advertising can no longer dictate your choices. In this way you begin to direct your dispersed energies towards leaving your own unique legacy on this planet. Your trellis will support this movement, while also steadying you, and reminding you that we all live within limits. We cannot always be 'full on', trying to be everything to everyone. Instead, you will move from fear to faith, and force to source – you will more and more learn to just sit in.

SIT IN
Give up this sitting at life's edge,
this begging, earning, proving to belong.
Sit in full now; see how life supports you,
But not with things you bargained for.
Sit in,
Empty of those lists and rules,
all made from desperation.
The chains you wound around your soul,
which squeezed you in behind the lie,
that they would keep you from uncertainty.

Sit in, breathe in,
until another voice emerges,
And calls your name, though faint at first,
Until, shaky like a newborn,
With awkward steps, pure, unsure,
you stumble towards
A way of life,
that fits, and feels a lot like home.
(MARTINA LEHANE SHEEHAN)

PRESS PAUSE

Remember, your trellis for the soul must be built with some regular supportive and strengthening practices, ones which will help you to stay aligned to your core values.

Creating Your Trellis

Jot down what is staying with you from this chapter. Where might there be a personal invitation for you?

Journal about the things you need to say yes to, and where you need to say no. List those activities you might need to lessen, and those you might engage in more deeply.

Recognising that your life intersects with others, how will you leave your own unique trail behind you?

CHAPTER SEVEN
Ever Ancient, Ever New

Our role is no longer to merely ease suffering, bind up wounds, and feed the hungry, but through every form of effort to raise the powers of love upward to the next stage of consciousness.
(TEILHARD DE CHARDIN)

'YOU NEED TO SNIP THESE,' SAID JANE, ONE OF OUR community, pointing to a few of the big flowery blossoms on the rose bush. I trust her, when it comes to gardening, but now she is suggesting that I clip off these perfectly formed big bright roses. Bad enough that they are fastened to a trellis (yes, I still struggle with the trellis), now they are getting snipped and clipped. 'It is to help the new growth,' she explained. As bright and beautiful as they were, apparently they had taken over, and were impeding the growth of new little emerging buds. After they were snipped off, though I really missed the bright showy roses, I gradually began to notice that, just behind one of the drama queens, there lay some crimson buds, peering through and beginning to shyly unfold.

Sometimes the spectacular, the bright and showy parts of ourselves, has to be pruned for the sake of deeper growth. Even good things – good work and projects – in excess can obscure the buds of possibility.

This paring back forms part of the commitments taken in monastic life, which include vows of obedience, poverty, chastity, humility, hospitality, community and stability. Like stripping back the roses, the idea of vows can, at first, seem to be stripping life of its colour. They can seem quite restrictive and even negative, but when looked at in a more holistic way, they can be catalysts for growth and flourishing.

A VOW FOR THE NOW

Therefore every scribe who has been trained for the kingdom of heaven is like the master of a household who brings out of his treasure what is new and what is old. (MT 13:52)

Before you skip this chapter and assume that words like 'obedience' and 'stability' have nothing to offer to you, or to today's culture, let's look at them in a fresh way. Divesting them of any rigid legalistic definitions, we will explore how we can interpret some of them for contemporary living. We will look at them from a psycho-spiritual dimension. Let us suspend, for now, any preconceived associations we might have and allow ourselves to be surprised by how transformative some of the following practices can be.

OBEDIENCE

The word 'obedience' comes from the Latin *audire*, which means to 'hear' or to 'listen deeply'. The commitment to be obedient to deep listening, properly understood, can dispose us to hear what is trying to come to birth from within.

You cannot force open a bud; you cannot tell it to hurry on and open up. It remains obedient to its own timing. In the early summer, the little rosebud on the trellis outside our front porch appeared as if it would never budge. Its little petals were all curled in tightly, in need of more warming light before it could open. I found myself looking at it a lot, dreaming of what was to come. It taught me to wait, not passively but with intention and attention. It showed me how trustingly it rests on the trellis, leaning towards and basking in the light. It did not respond to my demands that it hurry up. Not in my time, but in its own inwardly directed time, something beautiful emerged, one petal at a time, until eventually there was a full blossoming of its gifts to the world.

The rosebud is obedient, not to the structure itself, but to its own inner law of life. This law is not external or imposed, but is indwelling with an intrinsic reaching towards life. Unfortunately, obedience to the structure has often become more important than commitment to the spirit underpinning it. We see this nowadays, when the diminution that threatens religious affiliation has provoked in some people, a kind of fundamentalist 'battening down the hatches' and closing doors to listening and dialogue. This fearful externalised allegiance to protect a structure is often to the detriment of inner discernment, or to any real growth and expansion.

We can spend a lifetime practising obedience to some spiritless structures, or we can hear the invitation to go deeper, to listen anew to where the spirit is moving, 'I am about to do a new thing; now it springs forth, do you not perceive it?' (Is 43:19). We need to practise a deep listening for the movements of the evolving life within, the new buds shyly unfolding in the spring and the surrender to letting go into autumn soil. Nature is often teaching us this deeper kind of obedience.

As I glanced out the window, several months after I noticed that first bud, I saw her. There she was in all her glory, fully flourished and sharing her bright crimson with the world. I lamented how, in my impatience, I had not witnessed her divine timing. I missed the uncurling of the petals; I just hadn't seen them, when tick-boxing my to-do lists and obsessing with the movie-making in my mind. Had I been so imprisoned by my busy life, silenced into servitude by life's constant demands, that I failed to see? And here she was, about to depart, sprinkling the garden with heaven's beauty, as many of her petals were already beginning to descend. They seemed to be whispering, 'let go, let go', as they danced through the air to return to the earth. I wished they would stay, as I desperately tried to hang onto summer. 'Not your timing, but mine,' the rose seemed to say, as she twirled through the air in flowing skirts of pink and red, whispering 'let go, let go'.

Only plastic flowers stay the same, and I didn't want a plastic life, so I vowed there and then that I would never force a bud to open, or never force a flower to stay. Below the surface of things there is another wisdom, just as the sun surrenders herself to the ascending moon, and the tree surrenders her autumn leaves to the earth. All of this teaches us that we must never force the arrivals or the departures in the inner seasons of the soul. We must simply stay attuned with the ear of the heart.

HOSPITALITY

Upon returning from the Aran Islands on the west coast of Ireland, having visited my friend Deirdre Ní Chinnéide, I was deeply touched by the hospitality, both of the people and the spirit of the island. I ached to live the way of life in which a key could be left on the door, people stopped to talk to each other and the pace of life slowed down enough to offer hospitality to fellow pilgrims on the road. I wanted to bring back home some of the beautiful sayings and blessings of hospitality that I had long forgotten, but which live on in the psyche. Some of those blessings are very rich, such as Go dté tú slán (May safety be with you), or Dia Dhuit (God be with you), and the reply Dia is Muire Dhuit (God and Mary be with you). These are surely much richer and more hospitable greetings than an occasional smiley face or thumbs up symbol on Facebook.

In the Celtic world, there is a tradition of offering hospitality to the stranger, believing that every guest who comes to the door is the face of Christ. Saint Brigid was particularly known for her spirit of hospitality. She considered an unexpected guest to be Christ in the guise of a visitor, and would always lay an extra place at her table. As scripture reminds us, 'Do not neglect to show hospitality to strangers, for by doing that some people have entertained angels without knowing it' (Heb 13:2). We show hospitality whenever we lower the volume of the television and attend to the unexpected phone call, or when we stop and talk to someone on the street despite really wanting to stay focused on our shopping list.

In our home we have made a commitment to the table of hospitality. On our wall we have the 'Celtic Rune of Hospitality':

We saw a stranger yesterday.
We put food in the eating place,
Drink in the drinking place,
Music in the listening place.
And in the sacred name of the triune God,
He blessed us and our house,
Our cattle and our dear ones.
As the lark says in her song,
'Often, often, often, goes Christ in the stranger's guise.'
(CELTIC RUNE OF HOSPITALITY)

The practice of offering hospitality can call us to a radical availability, a sort of living without knowing the day or the hour when the stranger might arrive. In the past, I tended to want strong boundaries and demarcation lines between home and work. I considered home to be the place where I closed the door to the outer world. Soon those doors were flung wide open, which, in turn, flung wide open the doors in my heart. Each Sunday evening, it has been a joy to see the door opening and our little community arriving for a time of meditation and scriptural reflection. Afterwards, the kettle is on, the scones are out of the oven and stories are shared. This offering of hospitality has nothing to do with a kind of martyr complex about what 'we do for others'; it is simply an offering of space, where we are all mutually enriched. In committing to the offering of hospitality, everyone is both a giver and a receiver.

Of course, offering hospitality externally is not the whole story. We need to offer hospitality internally, to those parts of ourselves that we have banished from the table in our own inner selves. We need to befriend and welcome back the strangers in our own psyche. (Later we will look at healing and integrating the shadow part of our personalities.)

CONVERSION

The Latin word *conversatio* means to 'turn around'. Other meanings include 'being broken and renewed', a 'reshaping of mind and heart'. All definitions suggest some willingness to be changed or challenged. My own interpretation of 'conversion' would be something like this: an ongoing willingness to allow life to transform us, shape us and turn us around. It invites us to be open to 'the other' in a way that accepts that they might expand our way of seeing or might offer us unexpected guidance. Being open to conversion is to never settle for the belief that it is too late to change, but instead to be willing to turn around and begin again, and again. Buddhists tell us that we need to have a 'beginner's mind', whereby we can never assume that a situation or person has nothing new to teach us. The Desert Fathers and Mothers frequently referred to themselves as 'beginners' on the spiritual journey. A beginner's mind holds a 360-degree openness to opportunities, situations and people that might invite us to conversion, to turn around.

I like train journeys because they provide a type of moving gallery and time to withdraw. So, here I was, beginning to indulge in a new book, adjusting my glasses (and adjusting my face to the don't-dare-come-near-me look) and beginning to stretch out, taking up the full length of both my own seat and the vacant one next to me. Heaven! Two whole hours without interruptions – or so I thought. A few minutes later, I heard my name being called from a seat behind me. I reluctantly turned around. It was somebody I had worked with a lifetime ago. She had what we called an 'awkward personality', so I was reluctant to connect with her. I smiled faintly back at her and picked up my book again to resume reading. It was then I remembered the commitment to conversion, so I decided to turn around and greet her properly. She asked if she could take the empty seat near me (a hellish experience for us introverts). A few hours later, we had discussed many things – the death of our parents, the journey of grief – and the conversation brought up some difficult unfinished business that was still lurking from our working days. I began to see her in a different light, and began to see how I, and others, had contributed to her being 'awkward'. In the process I met the awkward part of myself, the part that needed to be transformed and converted. More importantly, I learned that each person is fighting their own battles, wrestling with their own inner demons, and doing the best they can on any given day. Later that evening, when looking back on the day, I noticed a peaceful feeling emerging as a result of that unexpected conversion, which came about by simply turning around.

If you were to consider your life as a crucible of learning, a school of love, how might some of your present struggles and difficult relationships be invitations to conversion, opportunities to turn around and see something, or someone, in a new way?

STABILITY

One of our greatest sufferings comes from our continual craving to be somewhere else, and our perpetual longing to be like someone else. When we are in states of craving, we are rarely content with the right here, right now, the present moment. When we live between 'if onlys' and 'what ifs', the grass is always greener somewhere else. The advertising world frequently endorses these perpetuating states of disquiet, encouraging that deadly disease FOMO (fear of missing out). We are tempted to follow all sorts of escape routes to avoid the discomfort or the perceived scarcity of our own lives. What if, instead, we embraced and searched for the gift in the imperfect, yet inherently perfect, present moment?

Life can become much richer when we develop the resilience to 'stay with, be with' and not run away. A rule of stability invites us to stay with uncomfortable emotions like grief, anger and emptiness instead of continually trying to escape them. It can be transformative when we stay with, open to, and soften towards, whatever is present in the right here, right now.

Enclosed monastics make a commitment to stability in choosing to live in a specific place with a specific community and choose to adhere to specific practices that foster spiritual growth. Likewise, we might find spiritual growth when we choose to bloom where we are planted, with these imperfect people that we have to live and work with. Maybe all the material for your growth is actually here in this present moment, when you remain rooted in awareness. If we keep moving from one mood-altering escape to another, one relationship to another, we will remain enslaved to some illusory freedom, where we will always be chasing the fantasy of something better out there. We then miss the opportunity to work on deeper patterns and we miss the possibility of retrieving some lost parts of ourselves. Most of all, we miss learning how to love and find compassion for all that is imperfect yet beautiful, within and without. The commitment to stability does not mean, of course, that we stay at any cost in a place or with a person that is damaging to our integrity, but it does mean we become willing to stay with the difficulties, as potential seeds of transformation. 'Carry the cell with you' was the advice of the desert dwellers. What did they mean? Perhaps it suggests that we carry an inner stability, a place of steadiness that can neither be earned nor taken away. When you carry this inner cell of steadiness with you, you can return there at any time, even if just for a moment between the inhale and the exhale.

In the biblical account of Jesus in the boat (Mk 4:35), I often wonder what it was that allowed him to sit unperturbed by the strong swirling winds around him. Wouldn't it be lovely to be that Zen-like instead of getting startled by every passing 'storm' in the mind and all the winds of change around us? Wouldn't it be lovely to have that kind of inner stability, one that creates a more authentic yes and an authentic no in our daily lives. As the gospel says, 'Let your word be "Yes, Yes" or "No, No"' (Mt 5:37).

We all need a kind of spiritual chiropractic now and then. Consider how we sometimes need to get our physical body realigned if it is out of balance, requiring a chiropractor to give a gentle (and sometimes not so gentle) adjustment. We are usually told to follow this with daily stretches or exercises to keep it in balance. (We are told to do the exercises, not just to think about doing them!) Could it be likewise with our spiritual life? What exercises will strengthen our spiritual muscles of inner resilience and stability?

When you create an inner stability, you are less inclined to accept other people's definition of you. You then become less co-dependent and less inclined to need everyone's approval. When you create new boundaries, an inevitable separation occurs between your ego and that which truly serves your soul. There is both loss and gain in aligning yourself to a spiritual centre. Some people may say that you were more fun when you were all over the place, always agreeable, all things to all people. The gain comes when you feel more focused and alive, and no longer clogging the arteries of your soul or frying your mind with spiritual junk food.

In life's passing storms, may we return to the centre of stability where 'we live and move and have our being' (Acts 17:28).

HUMILITY

The word 'humility' is another that has often been misinterpreted. It comes from the Latin word *humus*, meaning 'earth', to be 'earthed' and 'grounded', and has nothing to do with self-depreciation. A humble disposition sets us free from states of both inferiority and superiority because it is a way of being at home in our own skin. When we practise humility, we know how to stand our ground.

When we are able to enjoy being at home with self and others, without competition, comparison or striving to outshine, we no longer need that exhausting drive to prove ourselves or put on a show. It allows us to see how wonderfully gifted we are, while also living within limitations. The gift of humility, being rooted in the earth of our being, reminds us that we are enough, and there is no need for spectacular performances or inflammatory words. It reminds us that we are each a precious and beautiful channel for Divine flow.

Interestingly, the Benedictine Rule describes humility in terms of a ladder, and says instead of climbing upwards, we need to climb downwards into the earth of our humanity. Saint Benedict says, 'To step downwards in humility is the way to lift our spirit up towards God.'[1] With the advancement of psychology, we sometimes describe this journey to humility as transcending the ego, or going beyond the persona, in order to descend into the real self. I particularly like the scriptural vision of the prophet Micah (6:8), which I feel could be a powerful rule of life for the leaders of today – at a spiritual and political level. It simply states, 'To act justly, to love tenderly and to walk humbly with your God.' To walk humbly upon the earth would be particularly relevant to all of us at this time when we are awakening to the care of Mother Earth, recognising creation is not a commodity, but a gift to be reverenced.

In the Old Testament, the Book of Exodus describes an encounter that Moses had one day while tending his flock on the mountainside. When he turned aside and saw the burning bush, he heard a voice say, 'Remove the sandals from your feet, for the place on which you are standing is holy ground' (Ex 3:5).

Many people speak about the weeks of lockdown as having brought an acute awareness of how beautiful our planet really is; they reclaimed a sense of awe in their lives. They began to recognise that we are surrounded by 'burning bushes' – in people's eyes, in the wild flowers, the creatures, in all of nature and in life's surprises. For a while, we were all like Moses; we removed our shoes, and in humility recognised that all is holy ground.

---

1. Beverly Lanzetta, *The Monk Within: Embracing a Sacred Way of Life*, Sebastopol, CA: Blue Sapphire Books, 2018, p. 211.

True humility will give you a feeling of lightness in your heart and in the swing of your arms, especially when you begin to feel how lovely it is to know it doesn't all depend on you. You do not have to be in charge all the time, or have to be the brightest or the biggest, but with bare feet, you can enjoy the dance on the clay of your *humus*. Humility is to know you are big enough to be co-creator of Divine power, and small enough to know your own place in the interconnected web of life in an expansive universe.

GENEROSITY

I haven't seen generosity mentioned in any traditional rule of life, so I am adding it because I think it is vital to living the abundant life. Generosity begins with ourselves, because if we are not generous with ourselves, we will not be generous with anyone. When we are mean-spirited towards the self, we become begrudging with others. When you allow yourself to experience true abundance, all is gift and you eventually begin to desire the same good fortune for others.

Dampening your joy or denying the gifts you have does not raise others up. So, maybe we should make generosity (to self and to others) a key commandment in life. Your overflowing cup does not take away from anyone else's fullness, because it is all coming from the one source.

IN CONCLUSION

Before we leave part one of this book, let us look again briefly at why we are exploring the benefits of creating a trellis as a contemporary rule of life. We are all guided by rules, most of them unconscious and working against, rather than for, our greater good. These unhelpful rules might, for example, be pressurising us to never say no to anyone or anything (except, of course, to ourselves). Victims of our own internal perfectionism, we become driven towards meeting the expectation of the status quo. This disconnects us from what matters most, and creates a type of psychological inflexibility that stunts our growth.

However, it is not wise to begin with guns blazing. Trying to change the whole thing at once means we get overwhelmed and end up changing nothing. We get so paralyzed that we just give up. The idea of creating this trellis for the soul empowers us to look first at what really matters, and then align our actions, attitudes, choices and pattern of living.

Remember, in committing to the values of your trellis, you will need to gradually expand your comfort zone, while remaining in your self-care zone, and avoiding pushing yourself into the panic zone. In this way, you begin to dissolve some of your autopilot ways of acting and reacting. In living more intentionally, you engage in ongoing discernment around what might lead you away, or lead you towards, a more balanced life.

PRESS PAUSE

Remember, it is important to begin with bringing acceptance to wherever we are right now. That is the only place from which we can make small changes. We tend to overwhelm ourselves by comparing where we are with where we perceive others to be. When we are in states of comparison, we are rarely content with the right here, right now, present moment. When we live between 'if onlys' and 'what ifs', the grass is always greener somewhere else.

Creating Your Trellis

Jot down what is staying with you from this chapter. Where might there be a personal invitation for you?

How might a commitment to stability, hospitality, conversion and obedience speak to your life?

Maybe list some other commitments and core values that are important. Some examples that will be explored in part two are: integrity, compassion, hospitality, relationship, justice, stability, well-being, success.

Remember, the integration of your spiritual values does not require you to go away into a monastery (unless you feel so inclined); it necessitates that amidst everyday activities you keep one ear attentively listening to the music rising from within.

So, how might you practise engaging more fully in the world, while remaining anchored on your trellis for the soul?

Making a Contract with Yourself

What is not started today is never finished tomorrow. (GOETHE)

IN PART ONE, WE HAVE BEEN EXPLORING THE IDEA OF pruning back, and redirecting our energy towards what is most life-giving. We have been uncovering what is important for cultivating soulfulness. All of this will lead to important choices; for example, if you discover that you treasure a life of gratitude, mindful living, contribution, compassion or simplicity, you will be more and more unsatisfied with a culture that upholds expediency and personal advancement as idols of success. Likewise, if you treasure inner peace, you may need to gradually let go of some battles that are not yours to fight. If authenticity is important, you might find yourself letting go of the need for public recognition, status and repudiation. With increased self-acceptance, you will find yourself letting go of the exhausted quest to establish and protect your good name, alongside all those inner pressures to be recognised, rewarded and approved of. Remember, all of this letting go is in the service of your growth; it is a refusal to shrink yourself into habits that your soul has already outgrown.

SMALL IS BEAUTIFUL
The mustard seed, though the smallest of all seeds, yet when it grows is the largest of garden plants and becomes a tree, so that the birds come and perch on its branches. (MT 13:31–32)

Remember, small actions can be the seeds of big changes, which will spur us on those days when we feel tired and demotivated. You might like to introduce a few simple, but profound, small actions, such as:

- Each day as soon as you put your feet on the ground, recite the simple words, 'Thank you.'

- Write five things you are grateful for in your journal each evening.
- Choose to do one simple daily act that involves a small risk, one that takes you beyond the edge of what is familiar. (Remember again, in stretching the comfort zone, you need to respect your self-care zone and avoid the panic zone!)
- Make a to-be list that includes spaces for life's unexpected surprises.
- Practise offering hospitality to the people you meet in the daily rounds: the person at the checkout, strangers on the train and, of course, the strangers that emerge from your own shadow.
- Practise sending blessings to those who challenge you.
- Bless the paths you didn't take, bless what has been 'unlived' so all becomes an opportunity to live more fully.
- Pause for the bell: throughout the day create your own bells/reflective pauses.
- Take time each day to savour the beauty of nature and earth's abundance.
- Listen to an uplifting piece of music each day, or read a poem.
- Look around and see where you can become an advocate for the weak, the voiceless (human, animal and plant).
- Practise a 'screen-free Sabbath' half day or full day, if you feel able.
- Create a gossip-free zone in your home or at work.
- Recycle and re-use.
- Practise meditation daily, perhaps using the method of centering prayer, which is discussed in chapter fifteen.
- Breathe deeply whenever waiting for the kettle to boil, the computer to power up, or the pedestrian lights to change.

After you have reflected on some small actions, and perhaps have also added some bigger commitments, it is best not to move the goalposts according to your emotional temperature. Waiting until you 'feel like it' doesn't usually work so well. Like the roses, you too need regular attention, nourishment and pruning. So, before moving to part two, consider sketching some commitments and practices you are willing to introduce. Do it in pencil because you will be amending and adding to it after completing part two.

You might like to create a little contract with yourself, perhaps guided by the following template.

MY PERSONAL CONTRACT

I ... am committing to a way of life that serves my soul, and also serves the highest good of the collective soul.

I understand that this will involve letting go of some old ideas and habits, and will involve daily habits and practices.

Therefore, I am committed to these small changes ...

- On a monthly basis ...
- On a weekly basis ...
- On a daily basis ...

PART TWO

LET GO

No more clinging now to smaller worlds,
The ones that kept you safe,
in tired routines and schedules
all made from fear,
the ones that choked the tender buds
shyly peering and unfolding
from the garden of your soul.

And if you yearn for life, the fullest life,
Then let these go;
the why of life's unfairness,
The tightly held position
about a world that owes you.

Let go those things you thought were life itself,
treasures guarded,
stored and counted
and hoarded for so long.
Let them yield,
like sun-kissed tender buds.

Let go
The writhing and the hiding from the wound,
That tender place that calls you home.
Then you will feel the taste of being awake
where you know again
the beauty of your being.

In letting go, the deepest things inside you
Recognise, that this is life,
the only life worth dying for.
(MARTINA LEHANE SHEEHAN)

CHAPTER EIGHT
Wellness and Mental Health

WELL-BEING AND MENTAL HEALTH WERE THEMES THAT kept appearing in the listening process. Most people said this would be of primary importance in creating a trellis for the soul.

Stress is one of the major maladies of our time. Many are time poor and fatigued in spirit. Of course, we do need a certain amount of stress, sometimes called 'eustress' (which is 'stress' with the Greek prefix *eu*, meaning 'good'). This 'good stress' moves us toward our goals, dreams and life purpose. Motivation towards a cause and a desire to assist the collective evolutionary path of consciousness is a noble thing. We are not meant to be static or stagnant. However, this does not mean rushing through life while continually pumping adrenaline, cortisol and other stress hormones through our bodies.

NOT ALL IN THE MIND

Anxiety, stress and fear can manifest in symptoms such as a racing heart, swirling thoughts and nausea. Stress is not 'all in the mind'; it is well and truly manifesting in our bodies. When we are 'in knots' in our mind, we develop neuromuscular contractions (knots) in the body. This can show up in tight shoulders, back pain and headaches. An anxious, stressed mind can make life seem like a continuous emergency. This will activate the sympathetic nervous system. If the sympathetic nervous system is active and unrelieved for a prolonged period of time, it can lead to adrenal burnout.

Firstly, you need to become aware; in fact, awareness with compassion is the key to any real transformation. We have a part of the brain, known as the amygdala, that alerts us to danger. This is part of our neurological and evolutionary wiring. Our prehistoric ancestors, in order to survive, had to be perpetually on the watch for danger. This meant they had to become slightly negatively biased, watching for what could go wrong more than for positive opportunities. Even though nowadays we are not usually in physical threat, we often feel we are in psychological threat. The sympathetic nervous system cannot distinguish between the two and the fight/flight/freeze response kicks in whether the danger is real or perceived. We become hyper vigilant and armour ourselves up, like the hedgehog, or we run away. The more embedded these reactions become, the deeper the habit becomes until it is our new 'normal'. Recently, in counselling, somebody described it as having 'an inner Velcro for negatives and Teflon for positives'.

In our counselling practice, we have noticed that there are three habits that seem to be strong contributors to stress: anticipatory anxiety, ruminating about the past, and social comparisons. Each of these habits keeps us disconnected from the present moment.

- ♦ Anticipatory anxiety is where you find yourself continually watching for danger and for what could, or might go wrong. Here you become over-strategised and find yourself getting worn out with endless 'what ifs'. You might be thinking things like *what if I can't afford it* or *what if people don't like me*.
- ♦ Ruminative anxiety is where you are going over and over some past event, caught in endless cycles of 'if only'. Here you find yourself thinking things like *if only I had kept my mouth shut* or *if only I had made a different decision*.
- ♦ Social comparative anxiety is when you are finding yourself falling short in comparison to how other

people appear. Social media can perpetuate this habit. You see your friends having an amazing holiday and your life suddenly appears so dull. You think things like *I wish I could be as smart, as confident, as organised.* Don't forget that when you compare, you despair!

Anticipatory anxiety, ruminative anxiety and social comparisons are all energy robbers, and all create stressful mental activity. This, of course, does not just stay in the mind, but affects every part of our lives. These states are called 'secondary suffering'. In other words, while there is 'primary suffering' in all of our lives (the un-fixables such as loss, death, illness), we add a second layer (secondary suffering) with our thought patterns. Primary suffering is, in most cases, unavoidable, but secondary suffering is usually optional.

FEELING IS HEALING

You can, over time, begin to witness, rather than engage in, these habitual patterns of secondary suffering. In this witnessing position, you become less snared by and less entangled with the stressful and anxious thoughts.

Instead of being caught in endless reactivity, obsessing or avoiding, you can slow down and gently open to the fear underneath the anxious mental loops. Yes, open to the fear, rather than run away! You can then bring a gentle acceptance to what's really going on. You will probably discover another deeper layer lying underneath all the drama of the mind. This deeper layer has uncomplicated legitimate feelings, usually around fear, sadness, loss or vulnerability. Uncovering this layer is important because this is where healing can begin. Here you can begin to treat this feeling with compassion, befriending it as you would a child. You simply allow a gentle listening space for the emotion and the sensation in the body (instead of being distracted by all the mental noise). Feeling is necessary for healing. We do not heal anything by going round and round in mind games and catastrophic thinking.

WEAKENING THE STRESS CYCLE

Each time you notice yourself getting caught in excessive mental activity, you can gently return to the present moment, to the breath and to the body. Sometimes labelling the mental activity helps to dis-identify. In this way, you are in touch with the stress but you are not being frozen by it. Remaining in the moment, in the body, in the senses is a much safer place than being caught in the stories in your head.

Personally, I find that trusting in and surrendering to Divine Providence are the best wellness boosters. In doing so, we gradually replace worry with trust, fear with faith, and ego with spirit. There is a well-known prayer that would be helpful to include in the practices for your trellis. It helps us to discern between primary and secondary suffering, guiding us to differentiate between those stressors we can do something about and those we simply need to surrender:

God grant us the serenity
To accept the things we cannot change,
Courage to change the things we can,
And the wisdom to know the difference.

SHORT-TERM PAIN, LONG-TERM GAIN

Because we tend to have a slight negative bias, we need to actively introduce practices that tilt us towards the positive. What can we do to redress the balance? While acknowledging that we still have that ancient, primitive dimension known as the 'reptilian brain', we can educate ourselves to know we have choices.

If, for example, you hold a value around mental health and you continually sell out on it by saying yes to everyone and everything, then you are inevitably saying no to yourself and your values. You might feel an initial discomfort in saying no, but the short-term unease is for the sake of long-term peace.

Sometimes, we have to sit with the discomfort of disappointing others in order to adhere to our deepest values. In such times, you might need to ask yourself, what is important enough for you to be willing to endure a temporary discomfort?

Because we often sabotage our deeper needs in all sorts of subtle ways, it helps to ask this question: Is this action bringing me closer to my values or further away from my values? For example, if justice is one of your values and it necessitates you speaking out in public, you might need to ask: What small step can I take that will stretch me for the sake of my values, but not overwhelm me through excessive vulnerability? For example, writing this book is important to me, so in order to keep my commitment to the daily writing, I have to endure the short-term discomfort of saying no to cooking and housework. (This is not ringing true for those who know how domestically challenged I am!)

SMALL, STRETCHING MOVES

Small steps prevent us from being overwhelmed. Let's say we start off eating healthily on Monday, telling ourselves we're being really good so far. In the background is the fear that later we might become really bad. This sort of rule about being good and bad can beat us up when we do slip. It then throws us into such shame that we feel defeated and probably resume scoffing our comfort food, promising ourselves that we will try to be good again when we get back on track next Monday morning. This cycle actually perpetuates the kind of dilemma that got us into this in the first place.

When creating a trellis for the soul, we need to be respectful of our limits and incorporate self-compassion, which acts as a buffer to these stress spirals. When we gently take small, stretching steps, we can break the see-saw of procrastination and the fantasy that it will all magically change next Monday. We have to be steadfast in gradually building and strengthening our resolve. Otherwise, we become what St Benedict in his rule of life referred to as 'sarabaites', those 'never tested by a rule, never taught by experience, they have never become like gold from furnace instead they are in nature soft as lead'. We become 'soft as lead' when we let our spiritual resilience weaken.

PROCEED WITH CAUTION

As you integrate wellness onto your trellis, perhaps it is important to remind yourself not to seek 'perfection'. There is a new type of pressure that comes with the advertising of 'wellness' nowadays and it creates a situation in which we must keep raising the bar so high that we end up feeling bad every time we're not feeling good. That kind of defeats the purpose, doesn't it? It works against what well-being really means.

I overheard a conversation in a health food shop recently. One lady, with a basket full of expensive health food, miracle remedies and supplements, was telling another that she had 'slipped again'. She was berating herself for neglecting her juicing regime. This invited an equally contrite confession from the other lady, who leaned in, looked around and in a low, shameful voice began to lament how she had also slipped and had 'gone back on the chocolate again'. She went on to describe how she had also fallen into the mortal habit of eating bread again. Their moods were downcast and eventually something in me started to examine my own conscience. Had I also 'slipped'? Was I absolutely sure I had no impure thoughts about chocolate when trying to stay on a diet of avocados and organic kale? Soon I was self-tracking every bite and, in a rigorous confession, I found myself scrupulously repenting of everything I had eaten and everything I had failed to eat.

Later that evening a stunning half-moon shone in the window. It took my breath away and even though its shape wasn't whole and complete, it was shining a smile that lit up the whole room and the whole world. 'Maybe I'm not perfectly whole or complete either and that's okay,' I told myself. So I put away the sugar-free, wheat-free, dairy-free vegan cracker and continued to smile back at the moon while munching a big fluffy slice of bread with lashings of butter. Just for tonight, of course – it will be wheatgrass and quinoa again tomorrow!

'Good enough' is a healthy yardstick for all areas of our lives. Wellness is more than a fit body; it is about what we are digesting in all areas of our lives, not just food. For example, what are we swallowing from media? What are we satisfying our spiritual hunger with? Wellness includes our capacity to embrace the gift of imperfection. Theologian and contemplative scholar, Beverly Lanzetta says, 'Contradiction and paradox are intrinsic to this life. It is possible to receive spiritual illuminations, and even be touched by mystical union, and still be a flawed and struggling personality. ... We should not be surprised that we still seek to be whole.'[1]

ENJOY YOUR IMPERFECTIONS

Consider giving a whole day towards acceptance of imperfection. When you look in the mirror in the morning, smile in acceptance of the wrinkles, the extra few pounds, or anything else you would normally tend to be critical of. For this one day, do not compare yourself to anyone, just bring acceptance to who you are and how you are, in the now. If you go for a walk, go without your Fitbit. Do not count your steps or your calories. Maybe don't count anything – just breathe! On that day, do not straighten any crooked cushion or rearrange an untidy bookshelf. Above all, do not try to straighten or rearrange the people in your life. See how you feel at the end of a day where you have practised appreciating the gift of imperfection.

---

1. Beverly Lanzetta, *The Monk Within: Embracing a Sacred Way of Life*, Sebastopol, CA: Blue Sapphire Books, 2018, p. 211.

PRESS PAUSE

Remember, we sabotage our wellness in all sorts of subtle ways. If, for example, we find ourselves scoffing comfort food and telling ourselves it will all change on Monday, we might instead look at one small action we can take right now. That action needs to stretch the comfort zone a little, but must not bully us into the panic zone. Rather than trying to reach perfection, aim for the 'good enough for now'.

Creating Your Trellis

Jot down what is staying with you from this chapter.

How can you expand a definition of wellness beyond the narrow emphasis around the attainment of a perfect body?

Draw or write what a more holistic image of well-being would look like for you. What is really important to you in terms of wellness?

Now ask yourself: what short-term discomforts am I willing to embrace for the sake of long-term well-being?

Write three ways you tend to self-sabotage by moving further away from your value of well-being. Name three things you can do to move closer to your value of well-being. Consider how these actions can become part of a lifestyle change, a trellis for the soul.

CHAPTER NINE
All of Creation: Caring for Our Lovely Earth

WILDFLOWER WONDER

Two white butterflies emerge from the wildflower patch in our garden. It is like a scene from the film *Dancing at Lughnasa*. They are dancing in circles to music created by a blackbird perched on the branch of the oak tree. The house martins swish forward from under the roof of the porch and join the dance. Sheila, the sparrow who is rearing her family in our kitchen extractor fan, is very busy as she flies around, in and out, doing her shopping. Our dog, Holly – the abbess of our community – watches on with an air of authority and vigilance. Even the annoying rabbit that nibbles our shrubs is now welcomed to the dance. My soul is on tiptoe – breathless in the face of all this beauty.

Eventually the sun dances a few final steps, shyly genuflects and closes her eyes softly as she departs for the day. Apart from a few small yellow-bellied birds saying their vespers, there is a new descending silence, a kind of emptiness that is throbbing with fullness.

The next day, the house martins (dropping their remains onto the wall) resume being a nuisance, and the rabbit returns to being just an annoying intruder eating our veg, yet I was glad I was there for the dance, and that my eyes were anointed and softened even for those few minutes.

Who is it, I asked, that is praying through white butterfly wings, yellow-bellied birds and *Ruah* breezes? Who is breathing through sister wildflower and brother blackbird? Who is it that prays through salty tears moistened with gratitude for poignant beauty – for what the poets might call intimations of eternity?

'Who is it that prays within me?' St Patrick asked as he tended to sheep on a lonely hillside. Tradition has it that he was once asked to describe his God and he said, 'God is of Heaven and earth, of sea and river, of sun and moon and stars, of the lofty mountain and the lowly valley ... His life is in all things, He makes all things live.'[1]

EARTH AWAKE

Earth is calling us to be awake, whether through a whisper from a wildflower or an invitation to join the dance of birds and butterflies around us, or to notice the feathery sweep of the artist's brush across a cloudy sky.

The Celts saw the Divine Presence as inhabiting lakes, forests, oceans and mountains. For them, all of creation was hallowed and filled with sacramental grace. The earth was not seen as a backdrop to be used and manipulated, but was considered to inhabit something of Divine Revelation having its own life and spirit. Closeness to wild animals was part of the life of the Celtic saints, many of whom believed that creatures brought us gifts from the other world.

Saint Kevin (496–618), the Celtic saint who lived in a cave on the side of a lake, was very close to the natural world. Tradition has it that an otter would regularly bring him fish to eat. One day, as he lifted his arms in prayer, a blackbird landed on his hand and laid her eggs. The saint remained still until the eggs hatched and the baby blackbirds safely emerged.

Likewise, St Brendan (486–578) spoke of white birds draping the branches of trees and joining him in praising God by chanting the words of the psalms with him. Saint

---

1. 'Confession of St Patrick' in Joseph Duffy, *Patrick in His Own Words*, Dublin: Veritas Publications, 2000.

Gobnait received confirmation of God's presence through the presence of nine white deer, while St Columbanus encountered the Divine through a squirrel.

On the first day of our Ruah project, we were a bit nervous and feeling the familiar 'Are we mad?' dilemma. Suddenly, just before people arrived, I heard Pat call from outside, 'Look who has arrived!' I ran out to welcome what I presumed was our first guest, but there was no sign of a car coming up the driveway. Confused, I looked around and there was Pat out the back, taking a photograph of a fox! 'It's a sign,' he said, pointing to Brother Fox, who was just behind our hedge. 'Doubting Martina' wasn't so sure, so later that day I decided to look up what Celtic spirituality had to say about the arrival of a fox: it is believe that the fox reveals itself during times of unpredictability, compelling you to tune into your senses and act on your decisions. I am not so sure about it being a sign, but if St Gobnait trusted nine white deer and St Columbanus trusted a squirrel, perhaps our foxy friend had something to say.

WAKING UP

Laudato Si', Pope Francis' groundbreaking encyclical letter on care for our common home, says, 'Soil, water, mountains: everything is, as it were, a caress of God' (84). Waking up to the wonder of creation also means waking up to the suffering of our planet. It is difficult to really admit to ourselves the damage we are doing to Mother Earth, and so we need to face this pain together, and to engage in a collective search for ways to respond. On our Ruah transformational programme, we explored ways in which we can together make small changes towards helping to create a more sustainable world. Participants of the programme felt drawn in various ways to respond, from increased recycling, to switching to fair-trade goods, buying locally produced food, planting trees, lessening fuel emissions, installing energy-efficient bulbs and avoiding the use of plastic.

We began by deepening our gratitude for earth's abundant gifts: life-giving water, fruitfulness of the soil, life-sustaining fresh air, and the beauty of plants and trees. Our hearts overflowed with gratitude and we each became determined to do our bit. None of us want, at the end of time, to regret that we were the generation that did nothing to stop the damage:

One regret dear world
That I am determined not to have
When I am lying on my deathbed is
That I did not kiss you enough. (HAFIZ)

INTERCONNECTED

We lived, for a couple of years, at the edge of the ocean on the cliffs of Ballycotton in East Cork. It was a wild and windy place. One cold night, as I was just about to draw the curtains and cosy up to the fire with my book, I was suddenly drawn to the world of silver outside the window. The moon on the sea was casting its spell and, though it was freezing cold and the fire beckoned, Pat and I headed out into the night and walked right up to the top of the cliff. We stood in silence, for what seemed like eternity, in a world awash with silver. We listened, without speaking, to the lapping of the ocean and the haunting stillness. Then we heard it: a deep inhale and an exhale, strong and deep, followed by a chorus of other inhales and exhales joining in unison. We watch in silence until we saw before us shiny, silvery silhouettes – a school of dolphins. They came right out to meet us. Hardly able to draw breath, we stood in awe in this liminal space from which we had truly received a gift. We felt transported to a place where spirit called to spirit, and another voice was speaking.

The interconnectedness of nature and humanity was an integral aspect of ancient teachings, from the time of philosophers like Aristotle and Plato. When other thinkers around the time of the Enlightenment emphasised proof as the only reliable yardstick, a paradigm of separation and dualism emerged.

Saint Thomas Aquinas, scientist and theologian, stated in *Summa Theologica*, 'Because [God's] goodness could not be adequately represented by one creature alone, he produced many and diverse creatures, that what was wanting to one in the representation of the divine goodness might be supplied by another.' He proposed a cosmology of the 'eternal law', an emphasis on the sacredness found in all things. Pope Francis, in *Laudato Si'*, highlights this by saying, 'Nature cannot be regarded as something separate from ourselves' (139). He says that we are to cultivate and guard the garden the Creator has given us.

We cannot but marvel at the delicate ecosystem – the network of communal relations – in which we are called to live responsively, accountably and joyfully with beings of every sort. We are not just passive spectators, but we are each co-creators in an unfolding, expanding universe.

WEB OF LIFE

Evolution unfolds through each of us as we share the planet with millions of other species. The universe was not always as it is presently, but has become more differentiated, and is still evolving. And so are we.

The ecological crisis is begging us to listen. It tells us that to avoid future extinction, we must repent of and reject a way of life that aborts what is groaning in creation. We need to be mindful that we are all impacting on one another through our interconnection in the awesome web of life. What we do to the web, we do to ourselves. No matter where the damage to the web occurs, we all feel it at some level. We, therefore, either flourish together or we stagnate together. Our common home is like a sister, St Francis of Assisi told us. We cannot ignore the plaintive call of our sister as she cries out in pain because of the harm inflicted on her. We know we are indebted to her as we receive her nourishment and breathe her air. In *Laudato Si'*, Pope Francis calls for an 'ecological conversion', advising that it would be a mistake to 'view other living beings as mere objects subjected to arbitrary human domination' (82). In Ruah, we try to be especially committed to cultivating and guarding our garden as a place that welcomes birds, butterflies and bees. We try to be mindful of the small everyday changes we can make to help care for the earth as our common home, refusing those habits of convenience that add anything toxic to the environment. We try to integrate simple practices, such as reminding ourselves of the gift of the fruits of the earth before and after each meal.

CIRCLE OF CARE

Our circle of care must extend to all of creation because at the very heart of the universe is the movement of inter-relational energy. Psychiatrist and theologian, Gerald May tells us that 'we are so intimately joined in Divine Mystery that when a single one of us falls, we are all wounded. And when a single one breathes freely and opens to the exquisitely painful ecstasy of love, we are all nourished.'[2] We probably discovered all of this interconnection most acutely through the arrival of the global Covid-19 pandemic. So, whether the one that falls is a human being, an animal or tree, whether we hear it echoing in our neighbourhood or from a far-off place, it is part of our family.

Researchers in quantum physics and science agree that the universe is an interconnected system, each part related to the other. It recognises that, essentially, we are all one, held together by invisible chords. For St Francis, the relationship of nature and ourselves is described in terms of sisterhood and brotherhood. Likewise for Pope Francis, who writes in *Laudato Si'*, 'Everything is related, and we human beings are united as brothers and sisters on a wonderful pilgrimage, woven together by the love God has for each of his creatures and which also unites us in fond affection with brother sun, sister moon, brother river and mother earth' (92).

This sense of the fellowship of all life occupies quite a substantial space in the Book of Job: 'But ask the animals, and they will teach you; the birds of the air, and they will tell you; ask the plants of the earth, and they will teach you; and

---

2. Gerald G. May, *Will and Spirit: A Contemplative Psychology*, SF: HarperOne, 1987, p. 321.

the fish of the sea will declare to you. Who among all these does not know that the hand of the Lord has done this? In his hand is the life of every living thing and the breath of every human being' (Job 12:7–10).

As St Paul sees it, redemption includes all of creation. He says that all nature waits with longing for the glory that is in store for all (Rm 8:19).

CARETAKERS

We are caretakers of the earth and not absolute owners; therefore, we cannot take the individualistic view, grasping profit and gain without a thought about the long-term loss to creation. A world view that is mechanistic and rationalistic at the expense of Mother Earth is no longer an option. Nothing happens only 'out there', because everything is connected. We cannot be unaffected when hearing about the extinction of so many species, the cutting out of the earth's lungs through deforestation or the removal of mountain tops for open-cast mining. Something in us must surely be affected at hearing about the rising levels of plastic in our oceans and the devastating effect this has on sea life.

While it is truly heartbreaking to see pollution of air, water and the destruction of biodiversity, there is also good news as people, young and old, becoming increasingly aware of and active in environmental causes. It is heartening to see so many people making eco-friendly changes in their lifestyles, such as assessing and actively lessening their carbon imprint. Most of all, it is wonderful to see people appreciating the beauty of nature, instead of viewing it as just something for self-interest and utility. There has been a gradual shift in people's mentalities happening over the past decade, away from consumerism and capitalism and towards simple living based on gratitude, abundant simplicity, non-violence to our earth and to all living beings. We can all integrate simple changes into our daily patterns of living and make this part of a contemporary rule of life. Some of the following practical application might be worth considering:

- Be a mindful consumer. Everything we buy has an impact on the environment. Before buying a product, consider asking the following: How was this product made? Was child labour used in its production? Did its manufacturing process produce pollution? Can the packaging be recycled?
- Instead of buying plastic bottled water, choose glass bottles and jars.
- Avoid using paper or plastic cups.
- Install energy-efficient bulbs in your home.
- Use recycled paper.
- Avoid the use of chemicals in your home and garden.

Perhaps most importantly of all, we should each renew our sense of wonder, amazement and awe for this wonderful universe. This will bring increased awareness of our interdependence in the ecosystem; the bee needs the flower and vice versa. In creating our own trellis for the soul, we could make a simple intention to endeavour not to be part of a throw-away culture. Perhaps the following blessing of non-violence could be said daily for all of life – the tiniest insect, the tree in the Amazon Rainforest, the child in the womb and the fish in the ocean:

May all beings be safe this day.
May all beings be protected this day.
May all beings be free this day.

PRESS PAUSE
Remember, our circle of care must extend to all of creation because at the very heart of the universe is the movement of inter-relational community.

124

Creating Your Trellis

Jot down what is staying with you from this chapter. Where might there be a personal invitation for you?

Consider integrating into your daily life a spirit of gratitude for all of creation. Choose one or two of the practical applications listed above.

Decide to do one thing today that future generations would thank you for.

CHAPTER TEN
Balanced Lifestyle

Go confidently in the direction of your dreams. Live the life you've imagined. As you simplify your life, the laws of the universe will be simple. (HENRY DAVID THOREAU)

Simplifying our lives is key to greater energy and balance, both within and without. We are seeing, before our eyes, the ripple effect of our lifestyle habits on ourselves and on our planet. However, becoming prophets of doom will not help the evolving of any new consciousness. It is important to remind ourselves that we are not completely powerless but can intentionally create an alternative ripple effect by changing aspects of our lifestyle.

Many of those we spoke to in the initial listening process, as well as those who come on our programmes, are seeking to strip back some of the artificiality of our competitive culture, with its idols of busyness, excess and speed.

Statio in monastic tradition is the deliberate pausing after one task is finished and before another is undertaken. It is the taking of a moment between moments. I presume, like myself, on many occasions you have discovered yourself at the top of the stairs with no clue what you went up there for. This happens when you are still mentally engaged in the previous task or conversation and didn't take a *statio* before tending to the new task on hand. In living like this, I usually find that instead of saving time I actually lose it. And I wonder why I often find my keys in the fridge!

We have fewer and fewer *statio* moments now that we are tied to our gadgets. Many are suffering from a new type of OCD – obsessive checking disorder. Just look around and see how many people are continuously checking texts, emails and social media while waiting at bus stops, in supermarkets and even while in conversation with others. It is easy to get into the habit of checking our phones every time there is a pause. Perhaps we could, instead, practise simply taking a breath.

MIND THE GAP

We can create little gaps for paying attention to the voice of soul and the whisperings beneath the noise of everyday living. We often fill these gaps with activity, distractions and endless words, yet it helps to remember that every beautiful piece of music has gaps between the notes, each poem has gaps between the words, and there is even a gap between the inhale and the exhale of the breath. Perhaps instead of checking social media or cramming in a quick text or phone call, we could pause and mind the gap.

WORK–LIFE BALANCE

Whenever I am facilitating leadership and organisational days for staff, work–life balance is the most pressing presenting issue. Many speak of arriving home from work physically but with their minds still whirring with events from the day, recycling issues. Few pause and make a conscious choice to arrive home and be fully present there. The fallout from this is that the people we live with only get the leftovers; a ratty mood, perhaps, or a distracted and divided presence.

There is an emerging collective cry in consciousness for a way of life that offers a more harmonious rhythm for body, mind, spirit and heart, one that balances work and rest, connectedness and solitude. Homeostasis is the natural tendency of the body to return to balance, but it cannot do this if there is no space between activities.

'I feel a bit guilty saying it, but I'm enjoying lockdown,' a client shared with me during a counselling session on Zoom. It was two weeks after the lockdown had begun. I was taken aback; extroverted and a high achiever, she worked hard and partied hard. She went on to describe how the slower pace was beginning to feel very healing for her. 'My hair is a mess. I live in a tracksuit. But I'm laughing a lot at silly things and simple things,' she said. When the constant push for more was punctured, she discovered herself returning to homeostasis.

LIFESTYLE CHANGES

It is heartening to see an increasing number of people being drawn to a life of simplicity, stillness and abundance, a philosophy based on 'less is more'. Most people have an intrinsic attraction to a more balanced lifestyle and, perhaps, even to a more contemplative rhythm of life, but often lack the language of expression or guidance to affirm that quest. A fast-food mentality can easily permeate every area of life. Consider how you might punctuate each day with deliberate pauses in order to restore balance and offer gratitude for your life, including your health, your senses and simple gifts like a warm bed, a relaxing cup of tea or the aroma of coffee on the brew. Perhaps you might be attracted to a regular digital detox, a period of time, even if just your morning coffee break, when you take a break from plugged-in life. We often tell ourselves we should be more organised, but maybe we just need less stuff to organise. This is not meant to be a punitive kind of self-denial but a deliberate time for rest, stillness and a more balanced rhythm of life.

A BALANCING ACT

In earlier chapters, I mentioned that the desert dwellers of the third and fourth centuries committed to a life of balance, believing the hurried life was an enemy to serenity. In the Desert tradition, the word for deeper inner stillness was *hesychia*. These desert dwellers sought to be uncluttered in mind and heart. They practised *watchfulness* and *apatheia*, cultivating avoidance of extremes. They sought freedom from what they called 'inordinate attachments' (over-identification with possessions, reputation or status). They advised that no one area of a person's life should be so invested in that other areas get neglected. They sought to keep contemplation and action in balance. The old Ignatian concept *agere contra*, which translates as to 'act against', was used to mean 'act against self' or to 'die to self'. This is a kind of language that we find unattractive nowadays; however, if we were to interpret this as a dying to the false self, we would see its relevance in a more holistic way. There are times when we all need to practise *agere contra*; for example, when we are overreaching in one area of our lives and neglecting other needs, especially when the ego wants to run the show.

Creating a trellis for the soul is about small choices. This is especially important when we feel overwhelmed. Saint Benedict, in the prologue of his rule, speaks of perseverance, 'As we progress in this way of life and faith, we shall run on the path of God's commandments, our hearts overflowing with the inexpressible delight of love.'

I rarely feel any 'inexpressible delight' when trying to break an old habit. For example, I have discovered a few comedies on Netflix that have become quite addictive. During lockdown I got into the habit of watching them late at night and, of course, felt exhausted, unfocused and out of balance the next day. I had to eventually choose short-term discomfort (turning off the TV) for the sake of long-term fulfilment (being alert the following morning). Maybe you have your own 'harmless habits' that throw you off balance?

TILTING THE BALANCE

Nothing tilts the balance away from the negative as much as self-compassion. This is especially necessary on those days when we start off with great expectations but gradually become so overwhelmed that we end up doing nothing.

Only when we apply the soothing balm of compassion can there be a melting of the inertia that freezes itself around the heart like a block of ice. The combination of self-compassion with the taking of small, achievable steps is very powerful in shedding any addictive habit. This will also help in counteracting the voice of the internal critic in all its impossible standards and expectations. Strengthening your capacity to endure discomfort for the sake of your values cultivates a type of resilience and self-mastery.

Commitment to a balanced lifestyle spurs us to keep going, especially on those days when we are unmotivated, distracted or listless. And this is true even if, with unsure steps and wobbly knees, you can take one small step, and then another.

Shedding coats of dead routines,
A frightened soul uncurls, uncoils,
Tender wound, reveals the seed
Life's longing for itself.

PRESS PAUSE

Homeostasis is the natural tendency of the body to return to balance, but it cannot do this if there is no space between activities and no space beneath the 'stuff'. How might you begin to travel more lightly, while remaining hopeful and available to life as it unfolds right now?

Creating Your Trellis

Choose an area of your life that you feel has become out of balance.

Identify one self-sabotaging habit contributing to this.

Now, write one action that might bring some short-term discomfort but will bring long-term fulfilment. Integrate this habit into the creation of your trellis for the soul.

CHAPTER ELEVEN
Soulful Living

WE EACH HAVE A NEED TO GROW IN DEPTH. OUR ROOTS
need to grow deeply into the soil of our being. The more
active our life is, the more we need to take time to burrow
deep and draw nourishment from the source of life itself.
Meister Eckhart, the German mystic (1260–1328), said the
soul has two faces, 'one is directed towards God and the
other towards your life'. He suggests that there is a monk in
all of us. The word 'monk', *monachos*, comes from the Greek
monos, meaning 'to be alone'. The word 'hermit' is derived
from the Latin *eremita*, meaning 'of the desert'. Monks and
hermits are found in all cultures – Tibetan, Zen Buddhism,
Jewish, Islamic and Christian. When the ground of our
being knows how to be in solitude, we can be 'of the desert'
even in crowded rooms. Soulful people bring forth ripples
that heal separateness. They bring a subtle vibration that
infuses the world around them with compassion, love and
depth.

SOULFUL ELDERS
We often hear of the ancient Desert Fathers but unfortunately
not so much about the Desert Mothers. Women such as
Amma Sarah, Theodora and Syncletica became 'elders',
sought after for their wisdom and guidance. Amma
Syncletica (270–350), who grew up in the city of Alexandria
in Egypt was rich and privileged, but her soul longed

for more. She was interested in the spiritual quest from early in her life. She was a solitary, yet deeply committed to the poor. She advised, 'There are many who live in the mountains and behave as if they were in town, and they are wasting their time. It is possible to be a solitary in one's mind while living in a crowd, and it is possible for one who is a solitary to live in the crowd of personal thoughts.'[1] The feminine side of Divine Wisdom must not be lost, because the feminine spirit (in both women and men) can intuit the breath of the spirit in complementary and unique ways.

There are many today who are solitaries in the mind while living in a crowd. They live at the edge, not in the desert as the ascetics of old, but at the countercultural edge of fleeting fads, popular 'group think', and sometimes social acceptability. Soulful Presence is vital for the world we live in today.

'Living from soul' is not contrary to our true nature, it simply means we will not give our all to anything, except that which we know to be a pearl of great price. We plumb the depths for what we truly value, knowing that this is where the treasure lies – and according to the gospel there our heart will be also (Mt 6:21).

MONASTICS IN THE CITY

The sun began its descent and the city lights below were coming into view, as I sat outside a cafe late in the evening. The place was bustling with sounds of conversation and music as people relaxed with a coffee or glass of wine after work. Suddenly, for some inexplicable reason, I began to have a deep sense that we were all one, intertwined and rooted in the sacred web of life. Some were in conversation; others, like hermits, were sitting in little snugs on their own, reading their iPads and books.

Suddenly, all of life, even in this noisy cafe, seemed to be providing an opportunity to live in the monastery of the soul. I hope that the real monks wouldn't call this a bit of a cheap

1. Beverly Lanzetta, *The Monk Within: Embracing a Sacred Way of Life*, Sebastopol, CA: Blue Sapphire Books, 2018, p. 35.

shot, this stealing of their hard-earned rule of monasticism, the one they live, day in, day out, rising at 5 a.m. and surrendering many of the world's luxuries. What would they think of a charlatan like me, enjoying a cappuccino and a croissant under a trillion twinkling city lights, while transporting the idea of monasticism onto living the good life in a bustling cafe. Yet, I believe there are many uncloaked monks and mystics working at checkouts in supermarkets, tending the sick in hospitals and driving delivery vans late at night. So, whether it is the mother getting up in the middle of the night to feed her child or the addict trying to kick the habit, all have an ache and a soul cry yearning for life.

BECOMING AWAKE

When we talk about living from a soulful place, we are really talking about being fully awake. While I have found my home within Christian monasticism, no tradition has the monopoly of monastic living. There are many others also digging beneath the rubble for ancient and timeless pearls of wisdom. Many, for example, go to France to visit and stay in a place called Plum Village, where a group of Buddhist monks live a meditative life. Its founder, Thich Nhat Hanh, a monk and global spiritual leader, is emphatic that spiritual practice is not a hideaway in a safe little shell protected from the world. He says, 'Monastic life is only a means. If the means do not serve, it becomes meaningless. If the sufferings do not shake you violently so that you come awake, you have some false peace which you enjoy in your shell.'[2] He believes soul-work has to include being awake to the sufferings of the world.

Doctor Bernadette Flanagan says in her book, *Embracing Solitude: Women and New Monasticism*, 'We are in the throes of the birth of a new expression of humanity's transcendent quest.'[3] Bernadette has been a great support in encouraging

---

2. Mary Lou Kownacki, OSB, *Peace is our Calling: Contemporary Monasticism and the Peace Movement*, PA: Benet Press, 1981, p. 60.
3. Bernadette Flanagan, *Embracing Solitude: Women and New Monasticism*, OR: Cascade Books, 2014, p. 16.

us to commence our monastic rhythm at Ruah. She is passionate about the new face of monasticism, one that can exist both inside and outside the monastery walls. She suggested that what we are doing in Ruah is a hopeful sign, what she calls 'the first shoots of a new Pentecost – rooted in contemplative wisdom, a shelter for the soulful seekers of these times'.

REACHING ACROSS WALLS

Some might feel monasteries are outdated remnants of an ancient era but, in fact, they continue to be a powerful sign and witness of a life orientated around soulful living. In one of the modules of the *Trellis for the Soul* transformational programme, we invited Br Padraig, a member of the Benedictine monastery of Glenstal Abbey, Co. Limerick, to speak. On listening to him, the participants discovered very strong parallels between how the monks seek to live daily life in the monastery and how they themselves seek to live everyday life. We dismantled quite a few monastery walls as we met each other beyond structures, in a new nuanced, nameless space. We all agreed that, while living in community is difficult, living in our inner communities, with the many facets we meet in ourselves each day, is perhaps the greatest of all challenges. Through our conversation with Padraig, it became clear that, whether or not we wear a monk's garment, we each need to 'take the habit' of offering compassion to the many facets of ourselves.

ALL ABOUT SOUL

When we speak of 'soul' we are usually referring to that immaterial essence that precedes and continues beyond our earthly lives. I'm not going to launch into some abstract definitions here because I would be neither able nor willing, except to attempt the following:

Soul is the dimension that connects us to meaning, value, transcendence and beauty. It is not an abstract or ethereal disconnection from everyday life. Living at the level of soul is to go beyond the pervasive 'prove yourself' world view. It is to go deeper than any cultural mindset that values your life only in terms of output.

The following are some responses from our participants to the question: What is soulful living?

- ◆ It is recognition of the divinity around us.
- ◆ Something immeasurable, not born of ego.
- ◆ It is the espousing of gratitude and awe. It is living in flow and trust in providence.
- ◆ A recognition that we are all connected and supported by the innate goodness in people.
- ◆ It is drawing life from some sacred source, a healing place, a relationship with God, a place that lives on in Heaven.

I cannot add or subtract to the list except to say it feels, for me, like a place that includes, yet lies deeper than, passing emotions. It is a consciousness of which I am aware sometimes in early mornings or when walking in nature. In these times I feel suffused with love-energy that is drawing creation forward and continually evolving the universe. Sometimes I sense it in the eyes of somebody sharing the pain of their story.

You cannot really 'get soul' but, when you least expect, it can 'get you'! It gets me sometimes when I see people reaching out to the poor, when I see a little bird foraging for peanuts in the basket in our back garden, or while fingering my prayer beads in my pocket. I am in touch with soul whenever Pat and I gather in the evening in our meditation room to light a candle and remember all those we encountered during the day. The soft light and the quiet of the evening seem to unveil the essence and the gift of each person that crossed our path that day.

Soul moments can grab us through the sudden welling up of awe at the miracle of life or while discovering an unexpected softening in the heart when someone shows compassion or forgiveness. Sometimes an awareness of a subtle soul dimension comes through a beautiful piece of music, or while reading a book that confirms a deep wisdom or simply through the sudden awareness of an answered prayer. Soul moments can come through stirrings of deep joy and through pathos and sadness. Recently I met a woman who had just surrendered her young husband into full-time care, following a stroke. The tears rolling down her face broke into and broke opened my heart. The space between us felt as if it was filled with soul. Often when sitting with somebody in counselling or spiritual accompaniment, I experience a 'place in the middle' that I can only describe as a 'soul place'. The more you let soul moments 'get you', the more others will catch it from you.

NOT JUST HOLY COMPARTMENTS

Sometimes we consign soul experiences into holy compartments. I have always found the world a bit difficult and frequently experience a kind of marginality when I meet others who seem to have it all together, especially when it comes to practical things. Friends used to jokingly call me Mystic Martina because I was happier in places of solitude – nature, monasteries, cathedrals – rather than in shops or offices. I am prone to sensory overload and, so, am always relieved to get away from traffic, supermarkets or built-up environments. I regain energy when I return to the more natural surroundings of green spaces. However, I am gradually learning that God is not just in serene surroundings.

I was returning from Wales after a blissful week giving a retreat in a monastery. The walled garden with the ruins of old monastic cells, the enormous ancient trees and the connection with the retreatants in contemplative silence had cocooned me for the week. But now, I was entering into the bustling sounds, overpowering lights, flashing screens and loud overhead announcements of the airport. I began to feel that familiar 'thing' in the gut, the feeling of being lost in foreign land. That dizzy feeling of disorientation and dissociation was slowing me down as I fumbled in vain to find my ticket and passport. Behind me I could hear the impatient throat clearing of those I was delaying in the queue. After I managed to get things together, I looked for somewhere to recover as I muttered to myself about these 'godless places and godless, impatient people'. I bought a coffee and a sandwich in the bar and went to pay, only to find myself once again delaying everyone, this time because I had no sterling. The cashier said, a bit impatiently, that he could not take euro. A lady sitting opposite, seeing my embarrassment, came over and cheerily said, 'Allow me to pay for this.' I protested at first and then went to thank her but she just smiled and, walking away, said, 'Enjoy.' My heart swelled with gratitude for this un-winged angel, who reminded me that God does not just live in monasteries, but also in noisy airports and in pubs – and everywhere in the circle of life.

While still feeling a bit 'monkish', Mystic Martina has gradually been kicked out of her ivory monasteries and thrust into a broader understanding of what it is to live with soul. There are in-between soul spaces offered to us each day, perhaps en route to work, waiting at pedestrian lights or for a delayed flight. Seen in this way, all of life can become imbued with deeper presence.

PRESS PAUSE

Remember, you cannot really 'get soul' but, when you least expect, it can 'get you'! The more you let soul moments 'get you', the more others will catch it from you.

The soulful way asks that you not give your all to anything except that which your heart knows to be the pearl of great price, 'For where your treasure is, there your heart will be also' (Mt 6:21).

Creating Your Trellis

What deep promises are you willing to make in order to protect the treasures that are important to you?

How can you ensure that spiritual practice and everyday life are not competing events, kept in separate compartments?

Name a few of the un-winged angels in your life. In what ways have they been there for you? Can you tell them? (Otherwise, they might never know!)

CHAPTER TWELVE
Sabbath: Time to Fill the Well

IN THE DAILY RUSH OF LIFE, WE ARE OFTEN JUST STEAMING ahead, keeping the show on the road. A cherry blossom can be a cathedral of prayer, but we miss the invitation while worshipping at the altar of efficiency, bowing before gods of reputation and respectability. When our minds are whirring about a future that may not happen or reliving a past that has already gone, we miss the call of nature, especially when the changing seasons beckon us to lie fallow for a while.

The Desert and Celtic monks honoured times and seasons, observing the rising and setting of the sun, the waxing and waning of the moon, the ebb and flow of the ocean. Their life was rhythmic. They tuned into nature's times for blossoming and bearing fruit, and times for resting and lying fallow. The changing seasons remind us that we need both work and rest. The word 'shabbat' (anglicised as 'sabbath') derives from the Hebrew verb *shavat*, which means 'to rest from labour'. In the Jewish/ Christian tradition, the Sabbath was designed for stillness, relaxation and thanksgiving.

The first book of the Old Testament tells us that God rested on the seventh day, simply to look at, enjoy and love all of creation. Sabbath is a quality of heart and mind that enables us to pause, to observe and to bring love and gratitude for everything that exists.

Jesus frequently took Sabbath times. He went off into the countryside and surrounded himself with nature. 'He went up on a mountainside by himself to pray. When evening came, he was there alone' (Mt 14:23).

'I've noticed how lovely the purple is in a full thistle,' a neighbour said one day when we met, both of us walking slowly along the road during the lockdown days of 2020. Generally, we just honked the horn of our cars or exchanged a few lines at the shop, usually about how busy we were and how we really must catch up some day. (And that 'some day', of course, never happened.) Now, with nowhere to go, we talked and listened. I discovered both the loveliness of a purple thistle and the loveliness of the blue in her eyes.

One of our Ruah commitments involves the reclaiming of Sabbath as a time to become aware of the blessings of the past week. We try to keep it screen-free for at least some of the day. This was extremely difficult at first; now we look forward to it. In fact, there is actually a relief in not always being wired in, plugged in and full on.

A GIFT TO YOURSELF

'Six days a week we wrestle with the world, wringing profit from the earth; on the Sabbath we especially care for the seed of eternity planted in the soul ... the seventh day is a palace in time which we build.'[1] Taking time to 'care for the seed of eternity planted in the soul' can become a gift to yourself and to the world. A field that has been allowed to rest and go fallow for a while produces a more abundant crop. So it is with you. When you regularly protect a time apart to rest from labour, and intentionally return to source, you will find yourself less inclined to crave external validation or stimulation. When, however, you are buffeted about by everyone's expectations, jaded and tired, the world around you becomes jaded and tired also. You see things then not as they are but as you are.

When we take time to fill up our own inner well, we are no longer begging others to 'fill us up'. Author and ecumenical teacher, Fr Richard Rohr talks about this filling up as a time

---

1. Beverly Lanzetta, *The Monk Within: Embracing a Sacred Way of Life*, Sebastopol, CA: Blue Sapphire Books, 2018, p. 213

when we let God call us by name to a deeper place: 'This is the peace that the world cannot give. But I promise you it is also the peace that the world cannot take from you. This peace doesn't come from anything we do right. We have to discover what we have always been in God. When we get to this place, we will know and love ourselves, in spite of all the negative and opposing evidence. It is the spacious place of the soul. To live there is to finally be at home.'[2]

TO BLESS AND BE BLESSED

Sabbath gives us a sanctuary of rest and a time for perspective, reminding us that we are human beings not human doings. By taking this time, we develop an inner capacity to be at home everywhere and nowhere, at home with both doing and non-doing. Sabbath can be the time when the scales fall from our eyes and we begin to see how blessed we really are. An intentional time set aside to remember blessings can be very healing. It allows gifts to take root and blossom in our hearts.

As humans, we tend to hold a slightly negative bias, meaning that we are inclined to watch for dangers in our lives rather than notice the blessings. You know what it's like: you might receive many compliments throughout the day, but it's the one negative comment that stays with you. You see the silver lining, but then you search furiously for the dark cloud behind it. Sabbath time gives us space for tilting that balance from negative to positive, where even mistakes can be viewed as opportunities.

When we are blessed, we feel as if our very being is affirmed, not because of something we did, but because of who we are. Maybe we need to reclaim the simple but profound practice of blessing ourselves. Our hearts are imbued with longing to discover the naked truth of our inner beauty, without mask or role. Maybe before our life on earth began, we rested deeply and securely in the light of pure being, and so each time we are blessed, something

---

2. Richard Rohr, *What the Mystics Know: Seven Pathways to Your Deeper Self*, NY: Crossroad Publishing, p. 97.

in us remembers that nourishing, warming light. We need to be reminded of this because on a daily basis we are often too encumbered to remember this deeper home, what the poet William Wordsworth refers to as 'the trailing cloud of glory that we came from':

Our birth is but a sleeping and a forgetting;
The Soul that rises with us, our life's Star,
Hath had elsewhere its setting,
And cometh from afar;
Not in entire forgetfulness
And not in utter nakedness,
But in trailing clouds of glory do we come
From God who is our home;
Heaven lies about us in our infancy.[3]

STREAM OF CONSCIOUSNESS

It was Sunday and I woke a bit cranky. It had been a busy week. I had given two workshops in Dublin, and Pat and I only finished giving a retreat in Galway last night. I was conscious of my many un-returned phone calls to people looking for counselling and spiritual direction. My head was a bit full, and, to make matters worse, we had forgotten to buy bread. I was tempted to go straight into emails and work on the backlog, but decided instead to keep the commitment I had made to having some Sabbath Space. So, instead of opening the computer, I went for a walk. Head down, walking along, I was still counting all the things that were going wrong: too many things to do; only one slice of bread, which I reckoned would be eaten before I returned; and now the sunshine was changing to drizzle. I went as far as the small nearby bridge, where I always pause to listen to the stream for a while. The gurgling of the water gradually brought me to my senses. Suddenly, awareness cascaded through me. I began to think of all those people who would

---

3. William Wordsworth, 'Ode: Intimations of Immortality from Recollections of Early Childhood', *William Wordsworth*, Stephen Gill (ed.), Oxford: Oxford University Press, 1984, pp. 297–9.

wake this morning wishing more than anything that their problems were as trivial as those on which I was presently dwelling. Perspective returned and I became very grateful that I stopped at that stream for some Sabbath Space. In halting the spiral of negatives, I was opened to a new stream of consciousness.

My walk back had a different rhythm; the swing of my arms gained a buoyancy as I reflected on all those emails offering opportunities to do the work that I love, meeting beautiful people who bless me and who share their inner lives with me. The drizzle felt soft on my skin, filling my cup to overflow, and I looked forward to arriving home to a warm house, for a warm cup of tea – and who knows maybe there would even be a half slice of warm buttery toast awaiting.

Like the prodigal son in the gospel (Lk 15:11–32), when we come to our senses, we remember all the blessings that we have received. We begin to see the invisible light behind the tapestry of our lives.

PILGRIMAGE

When people come to counselling or spiritual guidance, it is usually because they have encountered some of life's big questions and crossroads. They express the desire to take some Sabbath time from everyday concerns, and some choose to embark on a type of pilgrimage. This can be both an inward journey, a pilgrimage into the heart, or an external journey, involving time spent in an unfamiliar place of natural beauty. Places like these can become catalysts for a kenosis, a kind of self-emptying. The roaring sea or secluded beach or mountain edge can offer itself as a backdrop, inviting us to bring into awareness some of our own big questions.

I lived in Co. Galway in the west of Ireland for a few years and found myself regularly travelling to the northernmost edge of Co. Clare, a place called Flaggy Shore. I didn't know what was drawing me there, but I went there on my own quite regularly, in all weathers, just to walk for hours along the windy edge of this wild coastline. I frequently felt a bit odd heading off here, but this wild edge and roaring sea was doing something to me. There was nothing neat in this rugged, poetic expanse of wild grey sea, grey rock and grey sky. I don't know what I was trying to walk out of me, or weave into me. I only knew something was trying to both fill me up and empty me out, all at the same time. Wild grey energies were seeping into my black-and-white world view. As I walked deeper and deeper into a landscape beyond the edge of my comfort zone, the landscape was wrapping itself around my soul. Here there were no clear-cut answers, only the haunting sound of a world bigger and vaster than the limits of my mind, a wild and wonderful place. Although I didn't know then the Celtic concept of 'thin places' (where we become more aware of another dimension), I felt this pilgrimage was calling me to a more expansive vista, where I began to look at life from both sides.

EVERYDAY SABBATHS

The Kerry poet and philosopher, John Moriarty was known to have spent long periods in stillness and reflection, especially when close to nature in Connemara. When I was working in Co. Galway, I frequently attended his poetry and reflective evenings. These few lines, often spoken by him, continue to echo in my mind: 'Clear days bring the mountains to my doorstep, calm nights give the rivers their say; the wind puts its hand on my shoulders some evenings, I stop what I am doing and I go the soul's way.'[4]

There are times in the day, when we are called to leave what we are doing and for a few minutes go the soul's way. Perpetual craving for what we don't have while taking for granted what we do have is guaranteed to set the scene for unhappiness; however, when we take time and space to count our blessings, life can begin to feel like a banquet.

While daily routines can often feel dry and devoid of meaning, taking a Sabbath moment for gratitude and to

---

4. John Moriarty, *Nostos: An Autobiography*, Dublin: Lilliput Press, 2001, p. 491.

savour blessings can help bestow worth and beauty on what would otherwise be 'just another ordinary day'.

SAVED BY THE BELL

The monks in the monasteries take Sabbath rest from work regularly throughout the day. The bell reminds them to pause for Lauds (early morning), Sext (noon), Vespers (evening) and Compline (night). These provide space to praise and bless throughout the day. Maybe we too could integrate a bell of reminder for Sabbath Spaces in our daily and weekly rhythms; a bell for Lauds in our busy mornings or Compline before we enter sleep?

SIMPLE BLESSINGS THROUGHOUT THE DAY

We all need to create little rituals and circles of protection around us. The more sensitive we are, the more we need this protection because our sensitivity makes us prone to absorbing everyone's 'stuff'. We can, unknowingly, be allowing others to take up squatter's rights in our fragile psyche. Most of our interactions are operating at an unconscious level, so, although it may not be their intention, people are often draining us. Perhaps when you notice that your energy is being drained, you could gently remind yourself of a protective boundary and circle of light around you.

The Celtic Christians started and ended every day by blessing and protecting themselves. The 'Caim' was a ritual in which a circle of protection was drawn around a traveller before they embarked on a journey. Likewise, the 'Lorica' from the Gaelic Irish tradition was a ritual in which the shield of God was invoked to protect from all harmful forces. Saint Patrick's Breastplate is the best-known example of a Lorica, but there are many other examples, such as the Lorica of St Fursa. The Celts had blessings for land and for crops. Water was blessed with the energy of the Holy Spirit and sprinkled on the fields, on foreheads before sleep, on food before mealtimes, and on journeys of leaving and returning. There were blessings for milking cows, baking bread and lighting fires.

Simple rituals add a rich texture to ordinary life, helping us to take note of the magic in the moment and the 'other world' in this world. You can add these rituals into your daily routine, reminding you to offer and receive blessings from wherever you are, whether you are brushing your teeth, taking out the rubbish or doing the dishes. Perhaps we could recite a short prayer as part of an everyday activity, like washing our hands. Simple tasks become imbued with sacred energy when we pause to bless and be blessed.

The following are blessings that I wrote for our own home. Perhaps they would be appropriate for use in your home too.

A Blessing for Morning
Divine Presence, may I awaken fully to the mystery,
of this sacred gift, this new day, offering itself to me.
Protect me from all negative energies, within and without.
Encircle me and free me from all imbalances in mind, and heart,
Help me to notice the quiet blessings that arrive,
And so
May I, and all beings, be filled, this day, with Divine Light.

Before Meals
As I begin this meal, I give thanks,
for this time of slowing and pausing,
I give thanks for the hands that prepared the food,
the earth that yielded to become nourishment for us.
I pray for those who, this day, may be grieving the loss of a face at the table,
and those who do not have enough to eat this day.
I ask a blessing on them, and all of us, and on this food.
Amen.

Night-time Blessings
In Ruah we commit to a short time in the little meditation room each evening, just to reflect on the day in gratitude, and to send blessings to those we encountered during

the day. We pray for those who come to our minds and consciousness, those who taught, inspired, challenged and guided us during the day. We remember those we heard about in the news, those who lost lives and those who grieve them. We pray for victims of crime and injustice. We remember Mother Earth and the animals and creatures that need protection.

May a circle of blessings surround those I have met this day.
May they be encircled with the Three in One.
May peace weave itself around their hearts this night.
And at the close of this day, and the close of our eyes,
May we all sleep surrounded by the angels,
Encircling, protecting and blessing.
Amen.

PRESS PAUSE

Remember, Sabbath offers us space to tilt the balance from negative to positive. It can be the time when the scales fall from our eyes and we begin to see how blessed we really are.

Creating Your Trellis

Jot down what is staying with you from this chapter. Where might there be a personal invitation for you?

How will you create a balance that honours your need for Sabbath rest and your need to have a sense of contribution and service in your life?

Perhaps you might like to write your own blessings.

CHAPTER THIRTEEN
Community: Healing and Integration

WE, AS HUMAN BEINGS, HAVE AN INHERENT NEED FOR community. In recent years, with unusual weather events and most especially the Covid-19 pandemic, the rhythm of our lives has been disrupted. This has been extremely challenging but it has also caused many of us to rediscover our need for community.

On many rural roads, there are signs saying, 'Neighbourhood Watch.' These serve as warnings that the area is monitored for suspicious activity but wouldn't it be wonderful if 'Neighbourhood Watch' also included regular check-ins – not just in times of crisis – especially to the elderly, the sick and those living on their own?

THE NEED TO BELONG
Our need for belonging is an ancient instinct, dating back to when our prehistoric ancestors hunted together in groups. Back then, being in packs provided more safety and so this primitive tribal tendency is still instinctual within us. Nowadays, we do not need to travel in packs for survival, yet we have an inner knowing that we are all interdependent. Community provides shelter and room for growth, and within the protection of community our gifts can be brought more fully to life. Just as the symphony orchestra is made up of the interaction of instruments, all

responding in different ways to the same rhythm, so it is in community; each person responds in different ways to the same spirit.

COLLECTIVE WISDOM

Wisdom often emerges when two or more people gather together. Whenever I give a workshop or retreat, I leave a lot of unfilled spaces, knowing that something will be born through the collective sharing. I try not to wrap it all up in my preparation; instead, I leave spaces for the unexpected, because I believe there is a power of wisdom when people gather together. This wisdom comes from the in-between space. It is not totally of me, even though it sometimes flows through me. It is not totally of the group, even though it emerges from the group. This collective wisdom is like electricity, a dynamic energy that we plug into through the power of the sacred gathering. This miracle of community happens whenever there is a dissolving of psychological distancing and ego competitiveness. It can even happen online, as we have discovered in times when meeting in person is not possible.

Jesus, in his farewell discourse, expressed something similar when he asked the Father that those who believed in him 'may all be one ... I in them and you in me, that they may become completely one' (Jn 17:21, 23).

SHELTER FOR THE SOUL

We find our best selves when connected and in service to the dynamic relationship that exists between us. We are spiritually, biologically and cognitively wired to be in connection with others. On Maslow's hierarchy of needs, in which the essentials for living are outlined, 'belonging' is ranked third. Relationships can offer us that push from the womb of self-isolation. Our deepest purpose is realised when we place ourselves in the service of one another and contribute to the spiritual evolution of all. The Hebrew word for 'holy', *kadash*, can also be translate as 'other'. Viktor Frankl also speaks about 'other' when he says, 'I wish to stress that the true meaning of life is to be discovered in the world rather than within man or his own psyche, as though it were a closed system.'[1] Spiritual practice, therefore, cannot be just a private affair, with each of us aiming to be 'holy' on our own terms. It demands that we care for each other and offer one another care. This sense of otherness expands our empathy, joy and creativity much more than just taking care of number one. Any form of spirituality that is divorced from community life or detached from responsibility for our brothers and sisters is surly suspect. Contrary to the conventions of our individualistic culture, the big question 'Who am I?' cannot be answered just by looking in the mirror. Even Jesus consulted others in his quest for identity and purpose. He said, 'Who do people say that the Son of Man is?' (Mt 16:13) This question cannot fully be answered outside of relationship and community. Some pop psychology suggests that all we need to do is keep looking in the mirror and repeating, 'I love myself. I approve of myself.' They say it will heal all self-esteem problems. Remember again what we say in Cork when we don't believe something will work: 'Good luck with that one, girl!'

CALLED TO THE TABLE

Scripture gives us many metaphors for community identity, such as, one flock, one body, vine and branches. *The Trinity*, the fifteenth-century icon by Russian painter Andrei Rublev, depicts a table where the Triune God is sitting in community, looking outward towards the whole universe. Around this table there can be no place for exclusion: 'There is no longer Jew or Greek, there is no longer slave or free, there is no longer male and female; for all of you are one in Christ Jesus' (Gal 3:28). The fourth seat is empty, giving us the message that we are all being welcomed home to share this table with the Divine.

When I hear the word 'home', I envision a seat at the table, a teapot, a kettle on the boil, and a *céad míle fáilte*. The dictionary

---

1. Viktor E. Frankl, *Man's Search for Meaning*, London: Random House, 2004, p. 115.

definition of 'home' is, 'A place where something flourishes, is most typically found, or from which it originates.'[2] True community can be the place where we flourish, where we discover we are more than just a trinity of me, myself and I. Each of us becomes a type of midwife for the birthing of soul in one another. Often around the community table, things happen in deeper ways than in formal settings. These few words came to me when our little extended community had left after our reflection one Sunday evening:

Sitting round the table, connected to the circle,
Where hearts are linked
In ways the soul alone can feel.

There are thresholds here,
beyond the vision of the eye.
A holding space, where fears and tears are held
for those who went before us,
for those still on the way.

Where pilgrim feet can rest,
departing or returning.
A place for birthing dreams,
baptising newborn visions.

The circle; always moving, always present,
A shelter for the soul,
a place the heart calls home.
(MARTINA LEHANE SHEEHAN)

DOMESTIC CHURCH

Father Bede Griffiths, OSB, a leading thinker in the dialogue between Christianity and Hinduism, envisioned a new type of monastic order. He says, 'Some monks may live in monasteries, but increasingly the majority will live in

---

2. 'Home', Oxford Dictionaries, Oxford University Press, https://premium. oxforddictionaries.com/definition/english/home (accessed via Oxford Dictionaries Online on 24 September 2020)

their own homes or form small communities – a monastic order in the world.'[3] He goes on to describe how the main emphasis would not so much be on affiliation to the same organisation but, 'behind all words and gestures, behind all thoughts and feelings, there is an inner centre where we can meet one another in the presence of God ... not because we will it or demand it to be, but because we have been seized by the Divine Mystery, and drawn into another dimension of faith.'[4]

In Ruah, through the sharing of practices that enrich the spiritual journey, we see something of this 'monastic order in the world'. While we do not all share common affiliations and opinions about everything, we share a soul synthesis that transcends all creeds and beliefs. In this way, we can remain diverse but not divided. God forbid that we would morph into a holy huddle! We consider this domestic church as similar to how the Celtic Christian monks would invite others to join them in the rhythm and prayer of their sacred circles. Visitors would join in their way of life, share a simple meal and help with some work in the monastery or the garden. It is the same in Ruah: the doorbell rings and one of our community arrives, sometimes calling into our little meditation room for quiet time or popping out to the garden to check on the peas or carrots they have growing there. (If the produce is ready, they will pick some and share it with others in the community.) This simple practice may eventually activate the cellular multiplication of other similar grassroots communities. Even the Covid-19 pandemic didn't stop the deep need for community. When we couldn't continue to meet in person and instead offered the programmes and retreats online, the spirit continued to draw people together through global communities via Zoom and webinars. We are discovering that there is no real blueprint for any of this. When, together, we start walking on this road – the road appears.

3. Beverly Lanzetta, *The Monk Within: Embracing a Sacred Way of Life*, Sebastopol, CA: Blue Sapphire Books, 2018, p. 40.
4. Ibid., p. 41.

A DWELLING PLACE

When we dive deeper, we discover we are all intertwined at root level. Author Jack Finnegan advises, 'Christian spirituality is about communion in all its many forms and permutations; if communion is lost ... spirituality loses its Christian stamp.'[5] This reminds us that the great commandment is to love both my neighbour and myself. Yes, a simple and difficult call, especially when it comes to loving those who don't agree with us.

FROM ME TO WE

On our *Trellis for the Soul* transformational programme, we have one session on 'Healing and Integration'. On the morning of that day, we look at self-compassion and in the afternoon, we explore the theme of forgiving others. When we mentioned in the morning that we would be doing 'forgiveness' later, there was a subtle change of atmosphere, a sort of stiffening up. One participant said she had to leave early, another said that he had a funeral to attend, and soon others began to chime in. After a while, we all laughed as we realised what we were doing – avoiding the difficult theme of forgiveness.

We decided, therefore, to begin by looking at those inner parts of ourselves that we have turned into enemies. We thought that we might be better able to cope with the speck in our neighbour's eye if we first looked at the log in our own. After we had compassionately explored the shadow within ourselves, those parts we often disown in our inner communities, it was much easier to look at those we dislike in the outer community. By afternoon, we were ready to look at forgiveness and there was no mention of funerals. Somehow the deceased had returned from the dead – or maybe it was the buried parts in us that had returned from the dead.

---

5. Jack Finnegan, *The Audacity of Spirit: The Meaning and Shaping of Spirituality Today*, Dublin: Veritas Pubications, 2008, p. 356.

SHADOWY PLACES

The Desert and Celtic seekers of long ago learnt something about the darker parts of our being, what renowned psychologist, Carl Jung refers to as the 'shadow'. They hoped to do combat with the demons infesting the wastelands, but it did not take long for them to discover that the demons were actually within. The wastelands and wild places did, however, offer a stark setting for meeting the self. The rugged emptiness and solitude of these windy sites offered no escape from what they called 'wrestling with inner demons'.

Saint Kevin is supposed to have chosen a cell in the most shadowy part of Glendalough, near the lake. He wanted the external shadow of this landscape to help him stay with the inner places of darkness. Personally, I would rather read a good book on the subject of the shadow, while drinking a glass of wine and relaxing on a sunny beach somewhere.

The rediscovery of the forgotten and rejected inner self is a bit like the return of the prodigal within. Buddhists describe the journey of excavating forgotten parts of the self as rediscovering our 'original face'. Writer and contemplative, Thomas Merton says, 'For me to be a saint means to be myself. Therefore, the problem of sanctity and salvation is in fact the problem of finding out who I am and of discovering my true self.'[6] He goes on to differentiate between the true self and the false self, describing the false self as 'the exterior, empirical self, the psychological individuality who forms a kind of mask for the inner and hidden self'.[7]

The shadow contains everything that has been pushed out of awareness. It is the part I insist is 'not me'. The more we disown unwanted energy – anger, jealousy – the denser it becomes and the more it tries to run the show. Of course, we also repress positive energy, such as our gifts and capabilities, and this is contained within the shadow

6. Thomas Merton, *New Seeds of Contemplation*, NY: New Directions, 1972, p. 31.
7. Ibid., p. 279.

too. Repressing the shadow is very tiring because it takes a lot of energy to push down vital energies.

Carl Jung has written much about the shadow and the journey towards integration. Author Robert L. Moore explains, 'The darkness of unconsciousness is very strong, but the light of awareness pushes it back. In Jung's morality of awareness, the struggle for individualism is a struggle for light, a struggle to get conscious, to get more of your experience and personality out of the dark so it can be respected, loved, accepted and affirmed. The challenge is in relating consciously to the depth and complexity of who you are.'[8] As Rumi says:

Out beyond ideas of right and wrong
There is a field. I'll meet you there.
Where the soul lies down in the grass
Where the world is too full to talk about
Where the phrase 'each other' doesn't make sense.

HIDDEN TREASURES

Often, the place that we deem 'dark' is actually filled with gifts for our growth. One way we can excavate this gold is by noticing where, and with whom, we have strong reactions and projections. Could our projections contain aspects of ourselves that we refuse to acknowledge? As a friend of mine keeps saying: 'If you spot it, you got it!' Can we call back and welcome those split-off parts, especially if they have been banished from our inner circle of care? Instead of cursing the parts we dislike, can we bless them, cradle them in compassion and see what they could teach us?

We can integrate these energies through offering kindness and acceptance. After all, it was the absence of acceptance that banished these inner aspects of ourselves in the first place. We will need to create a new holding place, one large enough to offer hospitality to those sometimes wild and unruly parts that have been left crying outside the door of our hearts.

---

8. Robert L. Moore, *Facing the Dragon: Confronting Personal and Spiritual Grandiosity*, IL: Chiron Publications, 2003, pp. 35–6.

LETTING GO

In theory, we all believe in the idea of forgiveness – until we ourselves have been hurt. When we begin to let go of the grievance, we discover a gradual release in our own nervous system and the solar plexus (the area around the tummy). Needless to say, this goes against the ego, the part of us that keeps asking, 'Why should I?' It is not easy to pray for people who have hurt us, or those with whom we still have unfinished business; however, our hearts expand when we attempt to send them a blessing, not from ego to ego, or grievance to grievance, but from soul to soul. I wrote the following little blessing that I try to silently recite to anyone that I find difficult to forgive. Perhaps you may find it helpful also:

A BLESSING FOR SOMEONE WHO HAS HURT YOU
May you be free of the wounding we shared.
May I, too, be free.
May you be released from holding the source of my pain,
And may I also be released.
May you find your own path in the universe,
As I find mine, and if those paths are destined to meet,
may we greet one another as 'beloved'.
And if destiny, out of kindness, keeps us apart,
May we, in speech, and in thought,
Tread lightly on the heart and path of memory.
(MARTINA LEHANE SHEEHAN)

PRESS PAUSE

Remember, our deepest purpose is realised when we place ourselves in connection with and in service of others, offering hospitality, compassion and shelter to one another.

Creating Your Trellis

Jot down what is staying with you from this chapter. Where might there be a personal invitation for you?

Identify a part of your humanity that you have banished from your own table of belonging. It might be repressed anger, vulnerability or jealousy. Write a letter addressed to that part. See if you can offer it hospitality and compassion.

If there is someone you have exiled/cut off, consider writing a note of forgiveness to him or her. If you are not ready, you might write a letter that you will not send. This will help you to release some of the complicated emotions. See it as one step on the journey of forgiveness and towards setting yourself free.

CHAPTER FOURTEEN
Dying to Live: Liminal Spaces

THE INDIAN POET AND PHILOSOPHER, RABINDRANATH
Tagore says that we sometimes receive an unexpected
glimpse of something from beyond the veil. He writes,
'Suddenly in a minute, a veil seemed to be lifted from my
eyes. I found the world rapt in an inexpressible glory with its
waves of joy and beauty bursting and breaking on all sides.
The thick cloud of sorrow that lay on my heart in many
folds was pierced through and through by the light of the
world, which was everywhere radiant. There was nothing
and no one whom I did not love at that moment.'[1] This
unitive experience, when a veil is lifted, is not the monopoly
of saints, philosophers and mystics. Perhaps deep in all
of our souls, we have a sense of our interconnection with
those who have passed on and we have a desire to know
that they are 'everywhere radiant'.

HELD WITHIN THE WHOLE
Many of those we interviewed in the listening process, as
well as some of those in our home community, said they
find it difficult to find spaces to talk about their mortality
and emotions regarding death and grief. Some expressed
the desire to be able to talk about their loved ones who have
died, and to have more natural and everyday conversations
about them. Often when people speak about their grief, in

---

1. Rabindranath Tagore, *Value*, London: Unwin Brothers Ltd, 1951, p. 35;
   Karl Rahner, Servants of the Lord, NY: Herder and Herder, 1968, p. 152.

an attempt to circumvent our own discomfort, we might try to change the subject, to remind them of happy memories, or even to move them on to some imagined bright future.

The Celtic monks believed that there were certain 'thin places', which they regarded as thresholds between time and eternity. They had many rituals to honour death and dying, believing they were deeply connected to their ancestors. They used the Celtic knot as a symbol to portray this unifying connection, with everyone and everything held in the whole.

In Celtic Christianity there are no demarcation lines between time and eternity, spirit and matter. Everything visible provides an opportunity to encounter the invisible mystery. In this way, death is natural, because birth lives at the heart of death and so those who have passed on are still journeying with us. The communion of saints, therefore, is not an abstract theology but a visceral reality in our lives.

'Keep death before you daily,' the rule of St Benedict advises. To know the shortness of life is true wisdom, says the psalm: 'So teach us to count our days that we may gain a wise heart' (90:12). However, it's not trendy to talk about death and dying in this present fast-paced culture. We airbrush death from our lives and, so, we lessen our facility to live fully. Just as the sportsperson's passion increases in the second half of the competition, so it is with us. We live more passionately and intentionally when we know that time is finite.

BEYOND THE VEIL

Each November, we gather in our home to give thanks for the legacy of those we have known and loved, those who continue to journey with us from behind the veil. We honour their place in our lives, thanking them for continuing to be soul mates helping us to navigate life's terrain. We light candles, sing, and share poetry and stories, all in celebration that 'we are surrounded by so great a cloud of witnesses' (Heb 12:1). We even share thoughts and feelings about our own mortality and, far from it being uncomfortable, we find that often people don't want this enriching time to end. There is always so much still to share, even after we blow out the last candle.

At the time of year when we turn our clocks back and say goodbye to the long days of summer for another year, we prepare ourselves for the darker half of the year, when the northern hemisphere is turned away from the sun. In the Celtic tradition, the feast of Samhain marks the end of the harvest season and the beginning of winter. It was seen as a threshold time as we cross over one of the two great doorways of the Celtic year, which was divided into two seasons: the season of light and the season of dark. In the Celtic imagination, this was considered to be a 'thin time', when the veil between heaven and earth grew more transparent and the spirits of our ancestors walked freely between the two worlds. For them, all forms of letting go were a type of dying into a bigger freedom only to find a new belonging, a new homeland, a new invitation to evolve, expand and grow. On certain days, such as the feasts of All Saints and All Souls, the Celts set places at their tables as a mark of welcome and hospitality to those who may return from the spirit world to visit their earthly homes.

Like the Celts, we can begin to pay closer attention to cycles of rising and falling, birthing and dying, not just in the land but also in our hearts. Patterns in nature can teach us something about transitioning, letting go and in-between places. They remind us of all the ways we are continually transitioning between births and deaths.

UNSEEN BONDS

You may have been told that you have your mother's smile or your father's wit. We inherit many genetic traits, both good and bad, from previous generations. Our ancestors can, however, also pass on what has been unfinished – the unacknowledged grief or unnamed disappointments. Psychologist Carl Jung says that family wounds can be carried in our ancestral line. He says that each one of us, whether we are aware of it or not, carry these wounds, and that part of our journey is to become aware of and, so, begin to heal these residual energies. What has remained unresolved and carried to the grave tends to get repeated. Often, what one generation works hard to bury, the next works hard to dig up. What was previously disowned or disembodied, the next generation is sometimes forced to own and to embody. Personally, I have had to undertake a long healing journey towards uncovering grief that I sense belongs to my deceased grandmother, whose name I bear. Though I never met her, I feel I carried her painful story in the cells of my being for most of my life. Nobody knew of her burial place and, for me, the fact that she was not named anywhere felt like a grave injustice (literally). Just as we were about to give up on ever finding it, our friend, Suzanne, discovered my grandmother's place of burial in an old newspaper archive. With great joy, we erected a plaque to her memory. I discovered, however, that I also had to release the skeletons of her past sufferings from their burial place in my psyche. Today, I feel she is a gentle guardian angel on my path.

We are all linked by unseen bonds. When we remember those we have loved and lost, we can, through the communion of saints, bring to light some of the unfinished scripts. We can allow the things unnamed and unsaid to emerge, not in a spirit of despair but in trust that the Spirit can heal across the span of time and eternity.

DYING INTO LIFE

Life's transitions can also be a kind of death; letting go of one stage to enter another. Perhaps, therefore, we cannot speak of death without looking at the death that the poor old ego has to regularly endure. The self-protective ego, with many tactics, resists any kind of dying and likes to cling to many false comforts. Scripture advise that 'unless a grain of wheat falls into the earth and dies, it remains just a single grain; but if it dies, it bears much fruit' (Jn 12:24). When we let something of the ego die and fall into the earth, a more creative, generous and expansive way emerges. We discover that 'losing our life' opens to become what we call the 'eternal life'. This is not something we have to passively wait for – the invitation to die and live more fully is here, right now.

Perhaps if we really glimpsed this, a lot of our fear would dismantle and we would no longer want to stay at the level of the ego mind. So, when we lose the argument, when someone else is better than us at something, when we are no longer in charge and running the show, maybe then, we are dying into life.

THE END PICTURE

'Starting with the end in mind' is a phrase often used in business training. It suggests that the end picture can tells us what steps we need to take right now. Maybe we could say the same about our lives. What end picture would you like?

We may as well start now, embracing the continuous 'little deaths', crossing thresholds from ego to spirit, fear to faith, tension to attention, from places that have grown too small and shabby for the soul. We discover that dying isn't just a future state but a place we already know deep in the soul.

It might help to ask whether, when it is all over, you will be able to say of your life:

Yes, I worked with what I was given. I tried to heal what limited me. I told my truth: sometimes I was loved for this, other times I was hated. I risked loving even when it meant losing. I risked losing when it meant loving. I relinquished safety and easy answers, and instead I poured myself into being the best version of myself that I could be.

PRESS PAUSE

Remember, this dying into life is not something we have to passively wait for – the invitation to die and live more fully is here, right now.

Creating Your Trellis

Jot down what is staying with you from this chapter. Where might there be a personal invitation for you?

How do you want to be remembered? What qualities would you want to be remembered for?

Rather than seeing these questions as morbid in any way, see them as prompts, helping you to keep the end picture in mind and to take another few steps towards what is really important in building your trellis for the soul.

CHAPTER FIFTEEN
Stillness, Meditation, Healing

But the silence in the mind
is when we live best, within
Listening distance of the silence
We call God.
(RS Thomas)[1]

I COULD NOT COUNT THE NUMBER OF PEOPLE WHO TELL ME they want to integrate a practice of meditation into their daily lives. The concept of mindfulness has become big business nowadays. It has been injected into business training, healthcare and education. This interest in mindful practices points to an emerging collective exhaustion from the goal-driven pace of our modern lives. When we put so much emphasis on craving and striving for personal advancement, we cultivate a perpetual disquiet and restlessness. Consequently, we now find ourselves searching for something to quiet our busy lives and busy minds.

BUSY MINDS
Author, scientist and pioneer of mindfulness programmes, Jon Kabat-Zinn emphasises the importance of recognising that we are more than the thinking part of our mind, saying, 'When you look at thoughts as just thoughts, purposefully

---

1. RS Thomas, 'But the Silence in the Mind', *Collected Later Poems 1988–2000*, Northumberland: Bloodaxe Books, 2004, p. 118.

not reacting to their content and to their emotional charge, you become at least a little freer from their attraction or repulsion.'[2] The busy mind is only one aspect of who we are but we tend to live habitually in that compartment, where the stale residues of yesterday invade and contaminate the freshness of today. This can be counteracted through creating a conscious intention to live each moment fully. We need to first develop an awareness around the constant stream of thoughts passing through the mind and, in so doing, can then become more free of the constant internal chatter. This practice can shed a light on the myriad of habitual and ruminative mental activities that continually prevent us from being present. In fact, the moment we notice that we are not present, we actually once again become present.

A more contemplative way of life teaches us to live mindfully, trusting that today's bread can only arrive today. This trains us to be less anxious and overloaded with tomorrow's problems, while creating acceptance around those many unfinished symphonies that make up our daily lives.

When we are paying full conscious attention to the present moment, we are no longer regretting the past or worrying about the future. Regular meditative practice can enhance brain function, increasing the grey matter associated with relaxation, awareness, empathy and attentiveness, as well as soothing those parts of the brain that produce stress hormones. Neurogenesis is a cutting-edge frontier of research and is a term used to describe how the brain, when given the right conditions, can rewire itself to embed our newly introduced cognitive states.

THE HAPPY BRAIN

During meditation, activity decreases in the part of the brain that activates the fight/flight/freeze response. Consequently, there is an increase of activity in the part

---

2. Jon Kabat-Zinn, *Full Catastrophe Living: How to Cope with Stress, Pain and Illness Using Mindfulness Meditation*, London: Piatkus, 1996, p. 342–3.

of the brain that triggers relaxation. This happens when, through meditation, you access the prefrontal cortex, which is the part of the brain that produces all that happy stuff, such as dopamine and serotonin. All of this can be measured scientifically as an increase in grey matter.

Regular meditation will help you to become aware that your internal mental chatter is not your essence. Only then can you begin to recognise yourself as the observer, not the victim, of your thoughts. The catastrophising or judging mind can then no longer encapsulate your reality. It cannot continue to hijack you by ruminating about the last conversation or rehearsing the next one. It is very liberating when you discover that the repetitive and often depressing thoughts in your head are not you.

MYSTIC HEARTS

In my work on retreats, many are interested in discerning the similarities and differences between the popular method of mindfulness and the practice of contemplative prayer. They also ask how they might integrate mindfulness with faith in God/Christ. This is an area in which I am very interested and have explored in detail in my previous book *Whispers in the Stillness: Mindfulness and Spiritual Awakening*.

I feel that the Contemplative Way, with its roots in the Desert and Celtic tradition, may be calling us again in this present mindfulness era. The desert dwellers fled from a place of collapsing institutional structures in order to cultivate a more contemplative way of living. Anthony the Great, often considered the father of the desert, suggested that just as a fish will die when it stays too long out of the water, so does our spirit die when we do not regularly tune into The Source. Perhaps when society disconnects from soul it dies at a fundamental level? Could there be a wake-up call here to all of us, and to organised religion, a call to shed some attachments to the externals and go deeper into the very core of the gospel?

Poustinia, the Russian word for 'place of solitude', has become popular again today. In my work, I am noticing an increase in the amount of people searching for *poustinia/* desert days, time out to practise and seek guidance to live mindfully. Interestingly, I am also noticing an increase in people coming for spiritual accompaniment/guidance. Traditionally, this was more a practice for those in religious life, but today there is an interest from a broad range of seekers, from inside and outside formal religious settings.

PRAYER

People often comment on how peaceful the little meditation room in our garden is. Yet, in truth, I occasionally have to drag myself there. Instead of spending time in its simple beauty, I sometimes distract myself with Internet browsing, TV channel switching or another cup of tea – anything but doing what the soul longs for. And it does truly long for it, as the lungs long for oxygen. Maybe prayer is difficult because we don't see or feel any result at the time. Maybe that's why the brain sends a message to the posterior, telling it to get up and do something more 'useful', instead of wasting time. Maybe it is difficult because during prayer, the 'doing' part of us is rendered redundant.

Despite my resistance, when I do give myself the time for meditation and prayer, I know I have come home, where the only thing I have to do is turn towards and bask in the gaze of Divine Love.

This intentional turning towards is not so much a seeking this or that, nor is it a desperate attempt to alter external circumstances. It is more a resting, a leaning into and a receiving of the warmth of Divine Love. It is a little space to leave behind the relentless to-do lists and enter the sanctuary of the inner room. Free of the compulsion towards analysing, measuring, evaluating or fixing, it is a burrowing down to a place deeper than the jumpy mind. In fact, the heart of prayer is less about thinking and more about resting. And rather like sunbathing, where we don't notice the tan (or freckles) evolving, later we see the subtle transformation.

Prayer is not another thing to 'do', nor is it just a speaking of words and gestures. It is an opening up and a reaching out of our whole being to be touched by the divine heart, which, of course, is already beating within us. In fact, when we pray, we discover, that all of creation dwells within our being, and the whole universe is somehow praying in and through us. For me, the relational dimension of prayer is crucial; otherwise, all disciplines and techniques are like empty crocks of gold at the rainbow's end.

RELATIONSHIP

When we experience the depths of ourselves, where we are silent and free of ego, we experience God. It is here we discover, not just who we are, but whose we are. Otherwise, religious practice is just a list of rules, and the gospel just an old story. Author and ecumenical teacher, Fr Richard Rohr emphasises this relational dimension to meditation, saying, 'Of course emptiness in and of itself isn't enough. The point of emptiness is to get ourselves out of the way so that Christ can fill us up. As soon as we are empty there is a place for Christ, because only then are we in any sense ready to recognise and accept Christ as the totally other, who is not me.'[3] He also says, 'God has become a Thou, and not just an energy field. And I have become an I, and not just a statistic. And the path is relationship itself and not just a practice, discipline or holy posture.'[4] Without the I-thou dimension, meditation can feel like an abyss.

CONTEMPLATIVE PRACTICES

We need a gentle trellis to help us stay present to the presence. In Ruah, we have two practices that act as a gentle trellis: Centering Prayer and Lectio Divina.

Centering Prayer

This is a meditative prayer that disposes us to receive the gift of contemplation. It calls us into a deep interior silence where the heart overflows and all words and images become

---

3. Richard Rohr, *What the Mystics Know: Seven Pathways to Your Deeper Self*, NY: Crossroad Publishing, p. 96.
4. Ibid., p. 84.

redundant. It has its roots in early Desert spirituality. Thomas Keating, a Cistercian monk who has pioneered the Contemplative Outreach movement, tells us it is a healing prayer, in which a transformation of the unconscious takes place. He describes it as 'Divine therapy'. Its simple guidelines are as follows:

- You sit comfortably and settle into stillness. Place your feet on ground, keep back erect and allow eyes to close softly. Allow yourself to breathe fully and naturally.
- Allow a sacred word to emerge and let it settle like a feather on the heart. This is not a mantra but a simple 'prayer word' that symbolises and holds your intention to consent to God's presence within. (It might be a word like 'peace', 'love', 'Jesus'.)
- Whenever you find yourself becoming engaged with thoughts, just return gently to the sacred word. You will, of course, be distracted many times with the busy mind and that's ok, just return to the breath, the present moment and the sacred word.
- At the end of the prayer period, remain and rest in silence for a while.
- Remember, the sacred word is not a mantra, and is only reintroduced whenever you get carried away with thoughts/distractions. It represents your consent to God's healing action for the full meditative period (which is usually about twenty minutes).

Lectio Divina (Sacred Reading)
This was the way of reflecting on the scriptures for the first thousand years of the early Christian Church. John, one of our participants in the weekly gathering, says, 'Lectio for me is a way of being, and a way of life that enables me to slow down and connect with myself, with God and with others. It is a continual spiritual process, a knowing that I am not alone.'

This way of reflection allows us to connect with the scriptures through our whole being and within the context of all of life. In Lectio Divina, we approach the gospel text as something alive, a love story written into the fabric of our lives and hearts, and not just seen as a tool to access information or a mere historical document. Through its distinct but interrelated movements (*lectio, meditatio* and *oratio*), we are allowing awareness to unfold gradually with the repetition in reading and reflecting on the text (throughout the week) becoming like background music.

SEAMLESS FLOW

These two practices, Centering Prayer and Lectio Divina, have stood the test of time across centuries and are still appealing to many today. They can be integrated into all of life in a seamless flow. You might consider exploring them a little further and integrating them into a rhythm of life for yourself.

Carving out time for either of the above practices can support us in entering more deeply into all of life. Again, let us remind ourselves that any method is only a finger pointing to the moon, not an end in itself. No matter how successful we are at any technique, if it does not lead to surrender and love, it is a lonely practice: 'I do not want to belong to a religion that cannot kneel. I do not want to live in a world where there is No One to adore. It is a lonely and laboured world if I am its only centre.'[5] Saint Teresa of Ávila reminds us, 'it is all about love melting into love' and we discover this through the presence in the present moment.

THE JOY OF THE NOW
The only life is Now, so, let's cease this striving,
driving, never arriving.
Let's rest in this imperfect, dappled now.
What if there's no longed-for future in tomorrow
And no perfect good old days.
The only life that's happening,
is already here, it's now.
What if you're already swimming,
In the sea of love you've longed for.
(MARTINA LEHANE SHEEHAN)

5. Ibid., p. 43.

PRESS PAUSE

Remember, choosing an intentional way of life, with deliberate times of solitude and withdrawal, is not a selfish activity. In prayer, the intentional 'turning towards', is not so much a seeking this or that, nor is it a desperate attempt to alter external circumstances. It is more a resting, a leaning into, and a willingness to receive the warmth of Divine Love.

Creating Your Trellis

Jot down what is staying with you from this chapter. Where might there be a personal invitation for you?

Take a few moments for quiet meditation. Allow a sacred word to emerge from within, let it rest like a feather on your heart. Allow this word to help you return to the present moment and to the presence in the moment. You could begin with just five minutes per day, ideally working up to twenty minutes. All you have to do is show up and allow God to do the rest. The sacred word holds your consent to rest in the transformative, healing presence.

CHAPTER SIXTEEN

Creative Expression: The Colour of Your Soul

Sometimes when you least expect,
she's there, Spirit Wisdom at your side.
She links your arm, and walks with you a while.
Then she cups your face so firmly,
That you glimpse your own reflection.
And you see those wasted years;
competing and performing,
for a world that never knew
the colour of your soul.

So, let's cease this endless search for signs of imperfection,
Where you forgot your home,
the land from which you came.

You must learn to dance again, she whispers softly
To the rhythm of a wilder, wiser you.
Only you can write the music of your song
Only you can wear
the colour of your soul.
(MARTINA LEHANE SHEEHAN)

CREATIVE EXPRESSION IS AN IMPORTANT PART OF building a trellis for the soul, because it adds glimpses of transcendence and beauty. Each of us carries the seeds of creativity within, yet we frequently hide away our potential for fear of ridicule. Often there are shimmering gems hidden in the rubble of the deeper self and when we excavate and share them, the world is a richer place. If we want to live a creative life, we have to let go of some of our feverish perfectionism and instead begin to practise being a beginner again and again. While not being an expert may be a little disturbing and threatening to our self-concept, we need to allow these new, and sometimes awkward and unfamiliar, energies into consciousness. We can welcome our nervous inner artist, poet, dancer or writer through regular simple practices like doodling, painting, photography and creative movement.

BORN TO BLOSSOM

Like the rose on the trellis, you are created to grow and blossom, but that requires the risk of opening up all that inner delicate beauty and sharing your colour with the world. Wouldn't it be so much safer to stay tight in a bud and insulated against the elements? Was it the invitation and nourishment of the sun against her petals that encouraged the rose to offer her generous scented gift to the world?

Staying tight in a bud is a real option; here we are more guaranteed to have protection and defences against life's unpredictability. But how much beauty would be lost to humankind? And what a loss for our own soul, because something in us knows we were born to blossom. Maybe you need to tell yourself just how amazing you are to have opened to life, again and again, despite the harsh winds and adverse circumstances.

THE DREAM IN THE SEED

In school many of us were asked what job we were going to do when we grew up. None of us were asked: What makes your heart sing? What is your deepest dream? What do you want to do with your one amazing opportunity to make a difference? It is a pity that these important questions are seldom asked because any attempt to override one's natural giftedness will always backfire, even if it conforms to the most virtuous or socially acceptable way of life. Deep inside, we know that the meaning of our life is related to discovering how to live our potential and how to add something beautiful to humanity.

The German Dominican mystic Meister Eckhart (1260–1328) says, 'You are God's seed. As the pear grows into the pear tree, and the hazel seed grows into the hazel tree, so does God's seed become God.'

There is an organic constellation of creativity imprinted in the seed of your soul. It has hints of how you might live a destiny that is unique to you, one that leaves a ripple in a world in desperate search for beauty. In leaving this ripple, you might not always receive the applause of society, but you will feel a deep fulfilment in your inner being. Our deepest calling, therefore, is to grow into our own authentic self-hood and to allow it to become a blessing for the many others who have forgotten who they are.

THE ARTISTIC MONK

The Celtic monks were known for offering creativity as service, illuminating and decorating manuscripts so that sacred texts would be protected. One of the delights of what we do in Ruah is offering afternoons of creative expression, where together we share music, poetry, film and ritual. As one participant said, on sharing the first poem she had ever written, 'It sort of flowed through me. It's as if the words were given to me from somewhere and, in writing them down, I was just the conduit.' She went on to say, 'I think the monk, the poet and the artist have a lot in common; they have to listen deeply to the spirit within.' When we access the core dream written in our hearts, we harness a life-giving energy that is like the mobilising of the acorn towards the oak, the sunflower towards the sun, the dancer towards the music.

Writing and doodling is my thing. Each morning, I go to my desk, sometimes still sleepy, to greet a fresh empty page. Usually, I have no idea what will emerge on that page, just as I have no idea what will emerge on that new day. It is both exciting and scary, energising and threatening, to be greeted by an unexpected visitor on the page. I have to follow where the pen takes me, even into realms for which I have no names.

Journaling, colouring and sketching can be powerful gifts, especially when dismantling some of our little agendas, those gauged too much towards popular opinion. The pen and page can pull our safer plans apart, telling us that our list is too tight, too certain, too small for the wildness of the spirit.

EMBRACING THE WILD

The word 'wild' means to be living or growing in a natural state. Maybe our wild side is the eternal part of us and all we let go is that which limits our eternal wildness.

'Putting out to sea' was an image of letting go that was much used by the Desert seekers and the Celtic Christians. In ancient Ireland, sometime between 512 and 530, St Brendan the Navigator set out in search of the Isle of the Blessed. Little was known at that time about anything existing out beyond the great horizon, but despite this uncertainty, some inner prompt was urging him to trust the current and let go of the known and the familiar.

There is a navigator in all of us, and we are hardwired for this letting go and evolving, from known to unknown, from control and ego attachments into the wildness of freedom. When the new is not yet in sight, we have to loosen our controls and simply trust the current.

LISTEN TO YOUR LIFE

Everyone, including you, wants to leave a meaningful ripple, a sort of creative trail, behind when they leave this planet. Anything less than this leaves a kind of gnawing pain in the soul. Parker Palmer, a great author, educator and activist, says you have to listen to your life: 'Vocation does not come from wilfulness. It comes from listening. I must listen to my life and try to understand what it is truly about – quite apart from what I would like it to be about – or my life will never represent anything real in the world, no matter how earnest my intentions.'[1]

LEFT NEEDS RIGHT

Most of the time we are using the left side of the brain to plan; making lists, organising events, controlling or solving issues. The human brain has two hemispheres and both need to work together and in balance. The left concerns itself more with the logical, the methodical and so prefers definitions, certainties and labels. The right brain is more concerned with creativity, possibility and intuitive knowing.

Left-brain activity is favoured in the business world, politics and in some church circles. We lose a lot of valuable creative wisdom when credence isn't also given to right-brain activity, the part that sees the bigger creative picture and can embrace, not just facts but also symbol, metaphor, imagination, intuition. Integrating this creative dimension may, indeed, slow down decision-making, but it usually leads to a more holistic solution. It may include having to embrace our complexities and contradictions as a creative force rather than seeing them as negative. We must allow these mysterious but creative aspects to come into conversation with our conscious self. In the gospel, Jesus rarely answered a question directly; instead, he looked across the countryside to find a symbol, a parable, a metaphor, a creative response. He pointed to the lilies in the field, the birds of the air or a grain of wheat. He saw things through a mystical lens because the logic brain cannot penetrate mystery. The mystic in us is awake to the beauty and poetry of every day. When expressions of spirituality lose this kind of mysticism and become overly left-brained, they become 'thrown out and trampled underfoot' (Mt 5:13).

GOD'S WILL

In the past, God's will was often an umbrella term for ignoring what you really want yourself. It suggested a kind

---

1. Parker Palmer, *Let Your Life Speak: Listening to the Voice of Vocation*, CA: Jossey-Bass, 2000, p. 25.

of contorting of yourself into somebody God supposedly wanted you to be. Even if it didn't suit you, you were encouraged to just 'suck it up'. As children, when serious sickness and tragedies frequently visited our home, and dreams were shattered, we were told, 'It's Gods will.' Needless to say that in such an environment, God's will could not possibly include such things as art, writing, poetry or dancing, and certainly not anything to do with fun. As a child, I used to love writing short stories, but stopped it abruptly when I was told that I was 'wasting paper and wasting time'. So, I interpreted that it was God's will that we suffered, but certainly not his will that we waste time with foolish things like writing, drawing or dancing. God's will was not good news.

I decided I had to do something about this, so I engaged my left brain and made a plan. I decided to gather the signatures of all those who would join with me in a protest against God. Yes, we were going to march against God! I reckoned this was an excellent plan, because if there were enough names collected, we would surely overthrow God and this miserable thing called God's will. I decided I would gather all the neighbours and even get the protest announced at Mass on Sunday. God will definitely have to back down now, I told myself. However, I wasn't too sure the following Sunday when I heard a sermon about sin and began to wonder if what I was doing might actually be a sin. Then I began to worry if it was mortal or venial. I reckoned if it were only a venial sin it would probably still be worth it in the long term. Besides, I consoled myself, it might not be a sin at all, after all I was only six years old, and so hadn't yet reached the age of reason.

I hope God laughed at the creativity of my plan – and perhaps is still laughing at the irony that I now give retreats and workshops on matters of spirituality.

Meister Eckhart, apparently, prayed to God that he could become free of God. Maybe in engineering that protest, I was also trying to become 'free of God' and the dodgy theology about what constituted God's will.

SEIZED BY DIVINE LOVE

Perhaps many of those who feel they have lost the faith are, in fact, attempting to become free of a false god, or maybe the old god is just too small. When we become seized by the presence of Divine Love, our spirituality becomes creative and alive. It is now something that can be felt and lived, and not just reasoned and intellectualised in the head. As Richard Rohr explains, 'The Incarnation had nothing to do with theology. It was rather about vulnerability, about letting go, about emptiness, about self-surrender – and none of that is in the head.'[2]

When you integrate an interior and embodied dimension to your spirituality, you begin to lay down old victim stances and take up the reins of responsibility for being a wild and wonderful co-creator. You discover that spirituality and creativity are of the one source, where all that is deepest within begins to flow like a river:

I believe in all that has never yet been spoken.
I want to free what waits within me
so that what no one has dared to wish for
may for once spring clear
without my contriving
If this is arrogant, God forgive me,
but, this is what I need to say
may what I do flow from me like a river,
no forcing and no holding back,
The way it is with children.
Then in these swelling and ebbing currents,
these deepening tides moving out, returning,
I will sing you as no one ever has,
streaming through widening channels
into the open sea.[3]

---

2. Richard Rohr, *What the Mystics Know: Seven Pathways to Your Deeper Self*, NY: Crossroad Publishing, p. 96.
3. Rainer Maria Rilke, *Rilke's Book of Hours: Love Poems to God*, Anita Barrows and Joanna Macy (trans.), NY: Riverhead Books, 1996, p. 58.

PRESS PAUSE

Remember, when we access the core dream written in our hearts, we harness a life-giving energy that is like the mobilising of the acorn towards the oak, the sunflower towards the sun, the dancer towards the music.

Creating Your Trellis

Jot down what is staying with you from this chapter. Where might there be a personal invitation for you?

Do you tend to operate predominately from left-brain activity (logic, facts, structure) or do you tend to give more credence to right-brain activity (the creative part that sees through symbol, intuition and the bigger picture)? Is there an imbalance and, if so, how might you integrate both left and right in a more holistic way?

Write freely about how you might allow some neglected part of your creative self to come into conversation with your conscious self.

CHAPTER SEVENTEEN
Launching Your Rule of Life

MOST OF US ARE SEEKING A WAY OF LIFE THAT IS AUTHENTIC, wholesome and joyful, while being of value and of service to the common good. There is a well-known story that suggests we have two wolves living inside our hearts. One wolf is bitter and negative and the other is kind, compassionate and joyful. They battle inside our hearts, but it is we, ourselves, who decide which one wins – through whichever one we feed the most. If we feed the kind, joyful, compassionate one, it grows stronger; consequently, the negative, bitter one weakens and fades. This demonstrates that we can intentionally feed and strengthen whatever qualities and values are important to us. We can feed the ones that create ripples of violence, hatred and war, or we can feed the ones that bring harmony, beauty and healing. Creating a trellis for the soul is essentially forming an intention to live an awakened life. It is a commitment to a set of practices that nourishes and strengthens that choice.

Even though there is a hedonic streak in us (the part that says just eat, drink and be merry), we are more than a bundle of instincts. *Eudaimonia*, something most of us desire, is the facility to hold discomfort for the sake of deeper growth, happiness and flourishing.

Psychologist Martin Seligman, who, since the year 2000, has been promoting this field of wellness and positive psychology, tells us that 'happiness is not just about obtaining momentary subjective states. Happiness also includes the idea that one's life has been authentic.'[1] He explored, in depth, those thoughts and behaviours that serve to give people a sense of purpose and balance and which, therefore, help to maintain people's sense of joy. His findings very much parallel what we discovered in our listening process, which has informed the guidance in this book. These practices include:

- Counting our blessings.
- Setting goals according to our values.
- Living in the present moment.
- Fostering social connections and community.
- Practising a faith that gives us meaning.
- Engagement in what contributes to the common good.

GUARDING THE SOUL

You can create your own energy through small actions, and the strengthening habits you practise. In tilting from the negative, you will need to continue to guard your soul from energies that can cause diminishment. You may, for example, have discovered that gossip, negativity and constant bad news infect you to the degree that you need to avoid certain situations. You may be more aware that even small choices affect your energy; for example, what you do to begin your day, the books you read and films you watch, the way you talk to yourself when you make a mistake, the people and situations you give most of your energy to, the thoughts you think before entering into sleep at night. Just as the recovering alcoholic has to avoid triggering situations or people, so it may be with you when you choose sobriety for the soul.

Creating a trellis is not an end in itself, but creates an anchor from which we can reach out more compassionately, and passionately, to a world in need of healing.

---

1. Martin Seligman, *Authentic Happiness: Using the New Positive Psychology to Realize Your Potential for Lasting Fulfilment*, NY: Free Press Publications, 2002, p. 262.

In balancing introversion with extroversion, you may find yourself seeking regular times of withdrawal to your inner monastery. You may need to do this in order to stabilise emotions and listen for divine guidance, so that you can offer your true self in service to the world. For a while you might appear a bit 'odd' to mainstream culture, but don't worry, that monkish oddity is also shared by poets, artists and anyone who has moved beyond the edge of the dictates of the status quo. You might find yourself moving a little slower, pausing a little more, complaining less, and even laughing to such an extent that others become curious about what you are up to. If that happens – bring it on!

A THORN IN THE SIDE
Divesting yourself of falsehood, you might become a thorn in the side of societal norms. Attracted to the need for reflection and space, some social events just won't fit anymore. While you might continue to go along with things for a while, just to blend in, after some time you will no longer force yourself to put up with situations that no longer sit comfortably with you. In honouring your primary commitments, you might find some relationships will grow stronger, while some will dwindle away.

Choices made from our most cherished values are inherently fulfilling because this is what sets us free from being puppets of circumstances. Perhaps this is most true when adversity strikes, because it is then we have to tap into qualities hitherto unused. If the spirit allows someone to be a red rag to your values, maybe it offers an opportunity for your inner bull to awaken. If it allows a Goliath to appear on your path, maybe it is because there is an undiscovered David within your soul. If there is a demon sent to taunt you, maybe it is because it brings forth the angel in your heart.

'THAT THING' THAT MATTERS
On finding one pearl of great value, he went and sold all that he had and bought it. (MT 13:46)

185

You have been exploring what is of most value to your life and now you need to look after it and look after your inner monk. Raimon Panikkar, scientist and theologian, says, 'The monk ultimately becomes monk not by a process of thinking, or merely desiring, but as the result of an urge, the fruit of an experience that eventually leads him to change and, in the final analysis, break something in his life for the sake of that "thing" which encompasses or transcends everything.'[2] Through the practices, you have been moving from just 'thinking or merely desiring' to creating a way of life for the sake of 'that thing' that matters most. Do you feel your personal challenge, at this time, in seeking to protect 'that thing' is to slow down a little or to become more active and involved?

Remember, in protecting the treasures of your soul, you will not seek to escape from the world, nor will you suddenly hold contempt for material goods, but you will be less addicted to such things for identity or mood alteration. None of this is about superiority to those who are less 'monkish'. In fact, the more authentic you become, the less superior you feel and the more you connect with your own fragility. The word 'fragile' comes from the Latin *frangere*, meaning 'to break'. Paradoxically, it is the broken parts that are often the entry point for the divine inflow. With this gift of fragility comes the gift of realising that it doesn't all depend on you.

This is your life
Wherever you are is the entry point.
(KABIR)

So, now, dear reader, it's over to you! Having explored the various themes in this book, begin to reflect on which are staying most strongly with you. Perhaps you could go back over all that you have written into your journal so far. You

---

2. Raimon Panikkar, quoted in, Beverly Lanzetta, *The Monk Within: Embracing a Sacred Way of Life*, Sebastopol, CA: Blue Sapphire Books, 2018, p. 27.

have already written a few commitments at the end of part one. The following envisioning questions will help you in the further development of your vision:

- What commitments are you willing to make in order to protect the treasures that are important?
- If you were to see yourself continuing to live a balanced life, true to your values, having a sense of contribution and service, what would this look like?
- What rhythms will you remain aligned with?
- What pace of living or social activities might you need to withdraw from?
- What will you engage in more deeply?
- What will you say no to? What will you say yes to?
- Who will support you and be your *Anam Cara* on the journey?

A CONSCIOUS CONTRACT

When crafting your contract, remember again the importance of stretching the comfort zone while staying within the self-care zone and avoiding the panic zone. Also, remember the importance of discerning between what is within your power to change, and what is outside your ability to control. You cannot, for example, change another person or their attitudes and choices. There may also be circumstances in your own life that you feel presently unable to change. However, you can alter your responses to these people and situations. You can, therefore, always make commitments around what is within your power. The following contract underpins how we try to live in Ruah. We use it as a kind of compass to discern whether we are staying true to our commitments. Perhaps it might spark something similar for you.

We are committed to living attentively to Divine Presence, through the practice of stillness, balanced lifestyle and ongoing discernment. We are committed to sharing the fruits of our contemplative practices through creatively expressing gospel values in a variety of soul-nourishing programmes in our home and through online events.

You might like to write your own vision statement, following this template:
I commit to ...
To ensure I stay committed to the above, I will continue to take these small steps:

- On a daily basis ...
- On a weekly basis ...
- On a monthly basis ...

Signature:

When you have completed and signed your commitment, put it in a visible place and maybe put an attractive colourful border or frame around it.

CONTINUING THE JOURNEY
And, on those days when you do not feel the sunlight, keep hope alive. Remember there is One who accompanies, guides and continually walks with you, whispering in your soul: *Keep going, keep growing, my lovely one, because you were created to flourish.*

BLOSSOM
May you awaken to the blossoming of your inner life
As you stretch your roots deep and wide
Raising your arms to the light

Make big moves now so
the world can see your splendour
As the beauty that has waited within
is awakening
offering love gifts to the world
strengthened by
Your trellis for the soul
(MARTINA LEHANE SHEEHAN)